WORKERS OF ALL COUNTRIES, UNITE!

J. V. STALIN

THE FOUNDATIONS
OF LENINISM

Lectures Delivered at the Sverdlov University

FOREIGN LANGUAGES PRESS
PEKING, 1975

Reprinted in 2010 by:
RED STAR PUBLISHERS, U.S.
www.RedStarPublishers.org

First Edition   1965
Second Edition   1975

PUBLISHER'S NOTE

The present translation of *The Foundations of Leninism*[1] is taken from the English edition of Stalin's *Works*, Foreign Languages Publishing House, Moscow, 1953, Vol. 6. Minor changes in the translation of the text have been made besides a few adjustments and additions in the notes at the end of the book.

Volume and page references to Lenin's *Works* made in the text are to the third Russian edition. English title references for the cited writings are given in the footnotes by the publisher.

DEDICATED
TO THE LENIN ENROLMENT

J. STALIN

CONTENTS

The foundations of Leninism is a big subject. To exhaust it a whole volume would be required. Indeed, a whole number of volumes would be required. Naturally, therefore, my lectures cannot be an exhaustive exposition of Leninism; at best they can only offer a concise synopsis of the foundations of Leninism. Nevertheless, I consider it useful to give this synopsis, in order to lay down some basic points of departure necessary for the successful study of Leninism.

Expounding the foundations of Leninism still does not mean expounding the basis of Lenin's world outlook. Lenin's world outlook and the foundations of Leninism are not identical in scope. Lenin was a Marxist, and Marxism is, of course, the basis of his world outlook. But from this it does not at all follow that an exposition of Leninism ought to begin with an exposition of the foundations of Marxism. To expound Leninism means to expound the distinctive and new in the works of Lenin that Lenin contributed to the general treasury of Marxism and that is naturally connected with his name. Only in this sense will I speak in my lectures of the foundations of Leninism.

And so, what is Leninism?

Some say that Leninism is the application of Marxism to the conditions that are peculiar to the situation in Russia. This definition contains a particle of truth, but not the whole truth by any means. Lenin, indeed, applied Marxism to Russian conditions, and applied it in a masterly way. But if Leninism were only the application of Marxism to the conditions that are peculiar to Russia it would be a purely national and only a national, a purely Russian and only a Russian, phenomenon. We know, however, that Leninism is not merely a Russian, but an international phenomenon rooted in the whole of

1

international development. That is why I think this definition suffers from one-sidedness.

Others say that Leninism is the revival of the revolutionary elements of Marxism of the forties of the nineteenth century, as distinct from the Marxism of subsequent years, when, it is alleged, it became moderate, non-revolutionary. If we disregard this foolish and vulgar division of the teachings of Marx into two parts, revolutionary and moderate, we must admit that even this totally inadequate and unsatisfactory definition contains a particle of truth. This particle of truth is that Lenin did indeed restore the revolutionary content of Marxism, which had been suppressed by the opportunists of the Second International. Still, that is but a particle of the truth. The whole truth about Leninism is that Leninism not only restored Marxism, but also took a step forward, developing Marxism further under the new conditions of capitalism and of the class struggle of the proletariat.

What, then, in the last analysis, is Leninism?

Leninism is Marxism of the era of imperialism and the proletarian revolution. To be more exact, Leninism is the theory and tactics of the proletarian revolution in general, the theory and tactics of the dictatorship of the proletariat in particular. Marx and Engels pursued their activities in the pre-revolutionary period (we have the proletarian revolution in mind), when developed imperialism did not yet exist, in the period of the proletarians' preparation for revolution, in the period when the proletarian revolution was not yet an immediate practical inevitability. But Lenin, the disciple of Marx and Engels, pursued his activities in the period of developed imperialism, in the period of the unfolding proletarian revolution, when the proletarian revolution had already triumphed in one country, had smashed bourgeois democracy and had ushered in the era of proletarian democracy, the era of the Soviets.

That is why Leninism is the further development of Marxism.

It is usual to point to the exceptionally militant and exceptionally revolutionary character of Leninism. This is quite correct. But this specific feature of Leninism is due to two causes: firstly, to the fact that Leninism emerged from the proletarian revolution, the imprint of which it cannot but bear; secondly, to the fact that it grew and became strong in clashes with the opportunism of the Second International, the fight against which was and remains an essential preliminary condition for a successful fight against capitalism. It must not be forgotten that between Marx and Engels, on the one hand, and Lenin, on the other, there lies a whole period of undivided domination of the opportunism of the Second International, and the ruthless struggle against this opportunism could not but constitute one of the most important tasks of Leninism.

I

THE HISTORICAL ROOTS OF LENINISM

Leninism grew up and took shape under the conditions of imperialism, when the contradictions of capitalism had reached an extreme point, when the proletarian revolution had become an immediate practical question, when the old period of preparation of the working class for revolution had come up and passed over to a new period, that of direct assault on capitalism.

Lenin called imperialism "moribund capitalism." Why? Because imperialism carries the contradictions of capitalism to their last bounds, to the extreme limit, beyond which revolution begins. Of these contradictions, there are three which must be regarded as the most important.

The *first contradiction* is the contradiction between labour and capital. Imperialism is the omnipotence of the monopolist trusts and syndicates, of the banks and the financial oligarchy, in the industrial countries. In the fight against this omnipotence, the customary methods of the working class – trade unions and cooperatives, parliamentary parties and the parliamentary struggle – have proved to be totally inadequate. Either place yourself at the mercy of capital, eke out a wretched existence as of old and sink lower and lower, or adopt a new weapon – this is the alternative imperialism puts before the vast masses of the proletariat. Imperialism brings the working class to revolution.

The *second contradiction* is the contradiction among the various financial groups and imperialist powers in their struggle for sources of raw materials, for foreign territory. Imperialism is the export of capital to the sources of raw materials, the frenzied struggle for monopolist possession of these sources, the struggle for a re-division of the already divided world, a struggle waged with particular fury by new financial groups and powers seeking a "place in the sun" against the old groups and powers, which cling tenaciously to what they have seized. This frenzied struggle among the various groups of capitalists is notable in that it includes as an inevitable element imperialist wars, wars for the annexation of foreign territory. This circumstance, in its turn, is notable in that it leads to the mutual weakening of the imperialists, to the weakening of the position of capitalism in general, to the acceleration of the advent of the proletarian revolution and to the practical necessity of this revolution.

The *third contradiction* is the contradiction between the handful of ruling, "civilised" nations and the hundreds of millions of the colonial and dependent peoples of the world. Imperialism is the most barefaced exploitation and the most inhumane oppression of hundreds of millions of people inhabiting vast colonies and dependent countries. The purpose of this exploitation and of this oppression is to squeeze out super-profits. But in exploiting these countries imperialism is compelled to build there railways, factories and mills, industrial and commercial centres. The appearance of a class of proletarians, the emergence of a native intelligentsia, the awakening of national consciousness, the growth of the liberation movement – such are the inevitable results of this "policy." The growth of the revolutionary movement in all colonies and dependent countries without exception clearly testifies to this fact. This circumstance is of importance for the proletariat inasmuch as it saps radically the position of capitalism by converting the colonies and dependent countries from reserves of imperialism into reserves of the proletarian revolution.

Such, in general, are the principal contradictions of imperialism which have converted the old, "flourishing" capitalism into moribund capitalism.

The significance of the imperialist war which broke out 10 years ago lies, among other things, in the fact that it gathered all these contradictions into a single knot and threw them on to the scales, thereby accelerating and facilitating the revolutionary battles of the proletariat.

In other words, imperialism was instrumental not only in making the revolution a practical inevitability, but also in creating favourable conditions for a direct assault on the citadels of capitalism.

Such was the international situation which gave birth to Leninism.

Some may say: this is all very well, but what has it to do with Russia, which was not and could not be a classical land of imperialism? What has it to do with Lenin, who worked primarily in Russia and for Russia? Why did Russia, of all countries, become the home of Leninism, the birthplace of the theory and tactics of the proletarian revolution?

Because Russia was the focus of all these contradictions of imperialism.

Because Russia, more than any other country, was pregnant with revolution, and she alone, therefore, was in a position to solve those contradictions in a revolutionary way.

To begin with, tsarist Russia was the home of every kind of oppression – capitalist, colonial and militarist – in its most inhuman and barbarous form. Who does not know that in Russia the omnipotence of capital was combined with the despotism of tsarism, the aggressiveness of Russian nationalism with tsarism's role of executioner in regard to the non-Russian peoples, the exploitation of entire regions – Turkey, Persia, China – with the seizure of these regions by tsarism, with wars of conquest? Lenin was right in saying that tsarism was "military-feudal imperialism." Tsarism was the concentration of the worst features of imperialism, raised to a high pitch.

To proceed. Tsarist Russia was a major reserve of Western imperialism, not only in the sense that it gave free entry to foreign capital, which controlled such basic branches of Russia's national economy as the fuel and metallurgical industries, but also in the sense that it could supply the Western imperialists with millions of soldiers. Remember the Russian army, fourteen million strong, which shed its blood on the imperialist fronts to safeguard the staggering profits of the British and French capitalists.

Further. Tsarism was not only the watchdog of imperialism in the east of Europe, but, in addition, it was the agent of Western imperialism for squeezing out of the population hundreds of millions by way of interest on loans obtained in Paris and London, Berlin and Brussels.

Finally, tsarism was a most faithful ally of Western imperialism in the partition of Turkey, Persia, China, etc. Who does not know that the imperialist war was waged by tsarism in alliance with the imperialists of the Entente, and that Russia was an essential element in that war?

That is why the interest of tsarism and of Western imperialism were interwoven and ultimately became merged in a single skein of imperialist interests.

Could Western imperialism resign itself to the loss of such a powerful support in the East and of such a rich reservoir of manpower and resources as old, tsarist, bourgeois Russia was without exerting all its strengths to wage a life-and-death struggle against the revolution in Russia, with the object of defending and preserving tsarism? Of course not.

But from this it follows that whoever wanted to strike at tsarism necessarily raised his hand against imperialism, whoever rose against tsarism had to rise against imperialism as well; for whoever was bent on overthrowing tsarism had to overthrow imperialism too, if he really intended not merely to defeat tsarism, but to make a clean sweep of it. Thus the revolution against tsarism verged on and had to pass into a revolution against imperialism, into a proletarian revolution.

Meanwhile, in Russia a tremendous popular revolution was rising, headed by the most revolutionary proletariat in the world, which possessed such an important ally as the revolutionary peasantry of Russia. Does it need proof that such a revolution could not stop half-way, that in the event of success it was bound to advance further and raise the banner of revolt against imperialism?

That is why Russia was bound to become the focus of the contradictions of imperialism, not only in the sense that it was in Russia that these contradictions were revealed most plainly, in view of their particularly repulsive and particularly intolerable character, and not only because Russia was a highly important prop of Western imperialism, connecting Western finance capital with the colonies in the East, but also because Russia was the only country in which there existed a real force capable of resolving the contradictions of imperialism in a revolutionary way.

From this it follows, however, that the revolution in Russia could not but become a proletarian revolution, that from its very inception it could not but assume an international character, and that, therefore, it could not but shake the very foundations of world imperialism.

Under these circumstances, could the Russian Communists confine their work within the narrow national bounds of the Russian revolution? Of course not. On the contrary, the whole situation, both internal (the profound revolutionary crisis) and external (the war), impelled them to go beyond these bounds in their work, to transfer the struggle to the international arena, to expose the ulcers of imperialism, to prove that the collapse of capitalism was inevitable, to smash social-chauvinism and social-pacifism, and, finally, to overthrow capitalism in their own country and to forge a new fighting weapon for the proletariat –

the theory and tactics of the proletarian revolution – in order to facilitate the task of overthrowing capitalism for the proletarians of all countries. Nor could the Russian Communists act otherwise, for only this path offered the chance of producing certain changes in the international situation which could safeguard Russia against the restoration of the bourgeois order.

That is why Russia became the home of Leninism, and why Lenin, the leader of the Russian Communists, became its creator.

The same thing, approximately, "happened" in the case of Russia and Lenin as in the case of Germany and Marx and Engels in the forties of the last century. Germany at that time was pregnant with bourgeois revolution just like Russia at the beginning of the twentieth century. Marx wrote at that time in the *Communist Manifesto*:

"The Communists turn their attention chiefly to Germany, because that country is on the eve of a bourgeois revolution that is bound to be carried out under more advanced conditions of European civilisation, and with a much more developed proletariat, than that of England was in the seventeenth, and of France in the eighteenth century, and because the bourgeois revolution in Germany will be but the prelude to an immediately following proletarian revolution."[2]

In other words, the centre of the revolutionary movement was shifting to Germany.

There can hardly be any doubt that it was this very circumstance, noted by Marx in the above-quoted passage, that served as the probable reason why it was precisely Germany that became the birthplace of scientific socialism and why the leaders of the German proletariat, Marx and Engels, became its creators.

The same, only to a still greater degree, must be said of Russia at the beginning of the twentieth century. Russia was then on the eve of a bourgeois revolution; she had to accomplish this revolution at a time when conditions in Europe were more advanced, and with a proletariat that was more developed than that of Germany in the forties of the nineteenth century (let alone Britain and France); moreover, all the evidence went to show that this revolution was bound to serve as a ferment and as a prelude to the proletarian revolution.

We cannot regard it as accidental that as early as 1902, when the Russian revolution was still in an embryonic state, Lenin wrote the prophetic words in his pamphlet *What Is To Be Done?*:

"History has now confronted us (i.e., the Russian Marxists – *J. St.*) with an immediate task which is the *most revolutionary* of all the *immediate* tasks that confront the proletariat of any country," and that ... "the fulfilment of this task, the destruction of the most powerful bulwark, not only of European, but also (it may now be said) of Asiatic reaction, would make the Russian proletariat the vanguard of the international revolutionary proletariat" (see Vol. IV, p. 382).

In other words, the centre of the revolutionary movement was bound to shift to Russia.

As we know, the course of the revolution in Russia has more than vindicated Lenin's prediction.

Is it surprising, after all this, that a country which has accomplished such a revolution and possesses such a proletariat should have been the birthplace of the theory and tactics of the proletarian revolution?

Is it surprising that Lenin, the leader of Russia's proletariat, became also the creator of this theory and tactics and the leader of the international proletariat?

II

METHOD

I have already said that between Marx and Engels on the one hand, and Lenin, on the other, there lies a whole period of domination of the opportunism of the Second International. For the sake of exactitude I must add that it is not the formal domination of opportunism I have in mind, but only its actual domination. Formally, the Second International was headed by "faithful" Marxists, by the "orthodox" – Kautsky and others. Actually, however, the main work of the Second International followed the line of opportunism. The opportunists adapted themselves to the bourgeoisie because of their adaptive, petty-bourgeois nature; the "orthodox," in their turn, adapted themselves to the opportunists in order to "preserve unity" with them, in the interests of "peace within the party." Thus the link between the policy of the bourgeois and the policy of the "orthodox" was closed, and, as a result, opportunism reigned supreme.

This was the period of the relatively peaceful development of capitalism, the pre-war period, so to speak, when the catastrophic contradictions of imperialism had not yet became so glaringly evident, when workers' economic strikes and trade unions were developing more or less "normally," when election campaigns and parliamentary groups yielded "dizzying" successes, when legal forms of struggle were lauded to the skies, and when it was thought that capitalism would be "killed" by legal means – in short, when the parties of the Second International were living in clover and had no inclination to think seriously about revolution, about the dictatorship of the proletariat, about the revolutionary education of the masses.

Instead of an integral revolutionary theory, there were contradictory theoretical postulates and fragments of theory, which were divorced from the actual revolutionary struggle of the masses and had been turned into threadbare dogmas. For the sake of appearances, Marx's theory was mentioned, of course, but only to rob it of its living, revolutionary spirit.

Instead of a revolutionary policy, there was flabby philistinism and sordid political bargaining, parliamentary diplomacy and parliamentary scheming. For the sake of appearances, of course, "revolutionary" resolutions and slogans were adopted, but only to be pigeonholed.

Instead of the party being trained and taught correct revolutionary tactics on the basis of its own mistakes, there was a studied evasion of vexed questions, which were glossed over and veiled. For the sake of appearances, of course, there was no objection to talking about vexed questions, but only in order to wind up with some sort of "elastic" resolution.

Such was the physiognomy of the Second International, its methods of work, its arsenal.

Meanwhile, a new period of imperialist wars and of revolutionary battles of the proletariat was approaching. The old methods of fighting were proving obviously inadequate and impotent in the face of the omnipotence of finance capital.

It became necessary to overhaul the entire activity of the Second International, its entire method of work, and to drive out all philistinism, narrow-mindedness, political scheming, renegacy, social-chauvinism and social-pacifism. It became necessary to examine the entire arsenal of the Second International, to throw out all that was rusty and antiquated, to forge new weapons. Without this preliminary work it was useless embarking upon war against capitalism. Without this work the proletariat ran the risk of finding itself inadequately armed, or even completely unarmed, in the future revolutionary battles.

The honour of bringing about this general overhauling and general cleansing of the Augean stables of the Second International fell to Leninism.

Such were the conditions under which the method of Leninism was born and hammered out.

What are the requirements of this method?

Firstly, the *testing* of the theoretical dogmas of the Second International in the crucible of the revolutionary struggle of the masses, in the crucible of living practice – that is to say, the restoration of the broken unity between theory and practice, the healing of the rift between them; for only in this way can a truly proletarian party armed with revolutionary theory be created.

Secondly, the *testing* of the policy of the parties of the Second International, not by their slogans and resolutions (which cannot be trusted), but by their deeds, by their actions; for only in this way can the confidence of the proletarian masses be won and deserved.

Thirdly, the *reorganisation* of all Party work on new revolutionary lines, with a view to training and preparing the masses for the revolutionary struggle; for only in this way can the masses be prepared for the proletarian revolution.

Fourthly, *self-criticism* within the proletarian parties, their education and training on the basis of their own mistakes; for only in this way can genuine cadres and genuine leaders of the Party be trained.

Such is the basis and substance of the method of Leninism.

How was this method applied in practice?

The opportunists of the Second International have a number of theoretical dogmas to which they always revert as their starting point. Let us take a few of these.

First dogma: concerning the conditions for the seizure of power by the proletariat. The opportunists assert that the proletariat cannot and ought not to take power unless it constitutes a majority in the country. No proofs are brought forward, for there are no proofs, either theoretical or practical, that can bear out this absurd thesis. Let us assume that this is so, Lenin replies to the gentlemen of the Second International; but suppose a historical situation has arisen (a war, an agrarian crisis, etc.) in which the proletariat, constituting a minority of the population, has an opportunity to rally around itself the vast majority of the labouring masses; why should it not take power then? Why should the proletariat not take advantage of a favourable international and internal situation to pierce the front of capital and hasten the general denouement? Did not Marx say as far back as the fifties of the last century that things could go "splendidly" with the proletarian revolution in Germany were it possible to back it by, so to speak, a "second edition of the Peasant War"?[3] Is it not a generally known fact that in those days the number of proletarians in Germany was relatively smaller than, for example, in Russia in 1917? Has not the practical experience of the Russian proletarian revolution shown that this favourite dogma of the heroes of the Second International is devoid of all vital significance for the proletariat? Is it not clear that the practical experience of the revolutionary struggle of the masses refutes and smashes this obsolete dogma?

Second dogma: the proletariat cannot retain power if it lacks an adequate number of trained cultural and administrative cadres capable of organising the administration of the country; these cadres must first be trained under capitalist conditions, and only then can power be taken. Let us assume that this is so, replies Lenin; but why not turn it this way: first take power, create favourable conditions for the development of the proletariat, and then proceed with seven-league strides to raise the cultural level of the labouring masses and train numerous cadres of leaders and administrators from among the workers? Has not Russian experience shown that the cadres of leaders recruited from the ranks of the workers develop a hundred times more rapidly and effectually under the rule of the proletariat than under the rule of capital? Is it not clear that the practical experience of the revolutionary struggle of the masses ruthlessly smashes this theoretical dogma of the opportunists too?

Third dogma: the proletariat cannot accept the method of the *political* general strike because it is unsound in theory (see Engels's criticism) and dangerous in practice (it may disturb the normal course of economic life in the country, it may deplete the coffers of the trade unions), and cannot serve as a substitute for parliamentary forms of struggle, which are the principal form of the class struggle of the proletariat. Very well, reply the Leninists; but, firstly, Engels did not criticise every kind of general strike. He only criticised a certain kind of general strike, namely, the *economic* general strike advocated by the Anarchists[4] *in place of* the political struggle of the proletariat. What has this to do with the method of the *political* general strike? Secondly, where and by whom has it ever been proved that the parliamentary form of struggle is the principal form of struggle of the proletariat? Does not the history of the revolutionary movement show that the parliamentary struggle is only a school for, and an auxiliary in, organising the extra-parliamentary struggle of the proletariat, that under capitalism the fundamental problems of the working-class movement are solved by force, by the direct struggle of the proletarian masses, their general strike, their uprising? Thirdly, who suggested that the method of the political general strike be substituted for the parliamentary struggle? Where and when have the supporters of the political general strike sought to substitute extra-parliamentary forms of struggle for parliamentary forms? Fourthly, has not the revolution in Russia shown that the *political* general strike is a highly important school for the proletarian revolution and an indispensable means of mobilising and organising the vast masses of the proletariat on the eve of storming the citadels of capitalism? Why then the philistine lamentations over the disturbance of the normal course of economic life and over the coffers of the trade unions? Is it not clear that the practical experience of the revolutionary struggle smashes this dogma of the opportunists too?

And so on and so forth.

This is why Lenin said that "revolutionary theory... is not a dogma," that it "assumes final shape only in close connection with the practical activity of a truly mass and truly revolutionary movement" ("*Left-Wing" Communism*[5]); for theory must serve practice, for "theory must answer the questions raised by practice" (*What the "Friends of the People" Are*[6]), for it must be tested by practical results.

As to the political slogans and the political resolutions of the parties of the Second International, it is sufficient to recall the history of the slogan "War against war" to realise how utterly false and utterly rotten are the political practices of these parties, which use pompous revolutionary slogans and resolutions to cloak their anti-revolutionary deeds. We all remember the pompous demonstrations of the Second International at the Basle Congress,[7] at which it threatened the imperialists with all the horrors of insurrection if they should dare to start a war, and with the menacing slogan "War against war." But who does not remember that some time after, on the very eve of the war, the Basle resolution was pigeonholed and the workers were given a new slogan – to exterminate each other for the glory of their capitalist fatherlands? Is it not clear that revolutionary slogans and resolutions are not worth a farthing unless backed by deeds? One need only contrast the Leninist policy of transforming the imperialist war into civil war with the treacherous policy of the Second International during the war to understand the utter baseness of the opportunist politicians and the full grandeur of the method of Leninism.

I cannot refrain from quoting at this point a passage from Lenin's book *The Proletarian Revolution and the Renegade Kautsky*, in which Lenin severely castigates an opportunist attempt by the leader of the Second International, K. Kautsky, to judge parties not by their deeds, but by their paper slogans and documents:

"Kautsky is pursuing a typically petty-bourgeois, philistine policy by pretending... *that putting forward a slogan* alters the position. The entire history of bourgeois democracy refutes this illusion; the bourgeois democrats have always advanced and still advance all sorts of 'slogans' in order to deceive the people. The point is to *test* their sincerity, to compare their words with their *deeds*, not to be satisfied with idealistic or charlatan *phrases*, but to get down to *class reality*" (see Vol. XXIII, p. 377).

There is no need to mention the fear the parties of the Second International have of self-criticism, their habit of concealing their mistakes, of glossing over vexed questions, of covering up their shortcomings by a deceptive show of well-being which blunts living thought and prevents the Party from deriving revolutionary training from its own mistakes – a habit which was ridiculed and pilloried by Lenin. Here is what Lenin wrote about self-criticism in proletarian parties in his pamphlet *"Left-Wing" Communism*:

"The attitude of a political party towards its own mistakes is one of the most important and surest ways of judging how earnest the party is and how it *in practice* fulfils its obligation towards its *class* and the toiling *masses*. Frankly admitting a mistake, ascertaining the reasons for it, analysing the circumstances which gave rise to it, and thoroughly discussing the means of correcting it – that is the earmark of a serious party; that is the way it should perform its duties, that is the way it should educate and train the *class*, and then the *masses*" (see Vol. XXV, p. 200).

Some say that the exposure of its own mistakes and self-criticism are dangerous for the Party because they may be used by the enemy against the party of the proletariat. Lenin regarded such objections as trivial and entirely wrong. Here is what he wrote on this subject as far back as 1904, in his pamphlet *One Step Forward*, when our Party was still weak and small:

"They (i.e., the opponents of the Marxists – *J. St.*) gloat and grimace over our controversies; and, of course, they will try to pick isolated passages from my pamphlet, which deals with the defects and shortcomings of our Party, and to use them for their own ends. The Russian Social-Democrats are already steeled enough in battle not to be perturbed by these pinpricks and to continue, in spite of them, their work of self-criticism and ruthless exposure of their own shortcomings, which will unquestionably and inevitably be overcome as the working-class movement grows" (see Vol. VI, p. 161).

Such, in general, are the characteristics features of the method of Leninism.

What is contained in Lenin's method was in the main already contained in the teachings of Marx, which, according to Marx himself, were "in essence critical and revolutionary."[8] It is precisely this critical and revolutionary spirit that pervades Lenin's method from beginning to end. But it would be wrong to suppose that Lenin's method is merely the restoration of the method of Marx. As a matter of fact, Lenin's method is not only the restoration of, but also the concretisation and further development of the critical and revolutionary method of Marx, of his materialist dialectics.

III

THEORY

From this theme I take three questions:

a) the importance of theory for the proletarian movement;

b) criticism of the "theory" of spontaneity;

c) the theory of the proletarian revolution.

1) *The importance of theory.* Some think that Leninism is the precedence of practice over theory in the sense that its main point is the translation of the Marxist theses into deeds, their "execution"; as for theory; it is alleged that Leninism is rather unconcerned about it. We know that Plekhanov time and again chaffed Lenin about his "unconcern" for theory, and particularly for philosophy. We also know that theory is not held in great favour by many present-day Leninist practical workers, particularly in view of the immense amount of practical work imposed upon them by the situation. I must declare that this more than odd opinion about Lenin and Leninism is quite wrong and bears no relation whatever to the truth; that the attempt of practical workers to brush theory aside runs counter to the whole spirit of Leninism and is fraught with serious dangers to the work.

Theory is the experience of the working-class movement in all countries taken in its general aspect. Of course, theory becomes purposeless if it is not connected with revolutionary practice, just as practice gropes in the dark if its path is not illumined by revolutionary theory. But theory can become a tremendous force in the working-class movement if it is built up in indissoluble connection with revolutionary practice; for theory, and theory alone, can give the movement confidence, the power of orientation, and an understanding of the inner relation of surrounding events; for it, and it alone, can help practice to realise not only how and in which direction classes are moving at the present time, but also how and in which direction they will move in the near future. None other than Lenin uttered and repeated scores of times the well-know thesis that:

"*Without a revolutionary theory there can be no revolutionary movement*" [my italics. – *J. St.*] (see Vol. IV, p. 380).*

Lenin, better than anyone else, understood the great importance of theory, particularly for a party such as ours, in view of the role of vanguard fighter of the international proletariat which has fallen to its lot, and in view of the complicated internal and international situation in which it finds itself. Foreseeing this special role of our Party as far back as 1902, he thought it necessary even then to point out that:

"*The role of vanguard fighter can be fulfilled only by a party that is guided by the most advanced theory*" (see Vol. IV, p. 380).

It scarcely needs proof that now, when Lenin's prediction about the role of our Party has come true, this thesis of Lenin's acquires special force and special importance.

Perhaps the most striking expression of the great importance which Lenin attached to theory is the fact that none other than Lenin undertook the very serious task of generalising, on the basis of materialist philosophy, the most important achievements of science from the time of Engels down to his own time, as well as of subjecting to comprehensive criticism the anti-materialistic trends among Marxists. Engels said of materialism: "With each epoch-making discovery... it has to change its form...."[9] It is well known that none other than Lenin accomplished this task for his own time in his remarkable work *Materialism and Empirio-Criticism*. It is well known that Plekhanov, who loved to chaff Lenin about his "unconcern" for

---

* "What Is To Be Done?", Autumn 1901-February 1902.

philosophy, did not even dare to make a serious attempt to undertake such a task.

2) *Criticism of the "theory" of spontaneity, or the role of the vanguard in the movement*. The "theory" of spontaneity is a theory of opportunism, a theory of worshipping the spontaneity of the labour movement, a theory which actually repudiates the leading role of the vanguard of the working class, of the party of the working class.

The theory of worshipping spontaneity is decidedly opposed to the revolutionary character of the working class movement; it is opposed to the movement taking the line of struggle against the foundations of capitalism; it is in favour of the movement proceeding exclusively along the line of "realisable" demands, of demands "acceptable" to capitalism; it is wholly in favour of the "line of least resistance." The theory of spontaneity is the ideology of trade unionism.

The theory of worshipping spontaneity is decidedly opposed to giving the spontaneous movement a politically conscious, planned character. It is opposed to the Party marching at the head of the working class, to the Party raising the masses to the level of political consciousness, to the Party leading the movement; it is in favour of the politically conscious elements of the movement not hindering the movement from taking its own course; it is in favour of the Party only heeding the spontaneous movement and dragging at the tail of it. The theory of spontaneity is the theory of belittling the role of the conscious element in the movement, the ideology of "khvostism" [tailism – *Red Star Publishers*], the logical basis of *all* opportunism.

In practice this theory, which appeared on the scene even before the first revolution in Russia, led its adherents, the so-called "Economists," to deny the need for an independent workers' party in Russia, to oppose the revolutionary struggle of the working class for the overthrow of tsarism, to preach a purely trade-unionist policy in the movement, and, in general, to surrender the labour movement to the hegemony of the liberal bourgeoisie.

The fight of the old *Iskra* and the brilliant criticism of the theory of "khvostism" in Lenin's pamphlet *What Is To Be Done?* not only smashed so-called "Economism," but also created the theoretical foundations for a truly revolutionary movement of the Russian working class.

Without this fight it would have been quite useless even to think of creating an independent workers' party in Russia and of its playing a leading part in the revolution.

But the theory of worshipping spontaneity is not an exclusively Russian phenomenon. It is extremely widespread – in a somewhat different form, it is true – in all parties of the Second International, without exception. I have in mind the so-called "productive forces" theory as debased by the leaders of the Second International, which justifies everything and conciliates everybody, which records facts and explains them after everyone has become sick and tired of them, and, having recorded them, rests content. Marx said that the materialist theory could not confine itself to explaining the world, that it must also change it.[10] But Kautsky and Co. are not concerned with this; they prefer to rest content with the first part of Marx's formula.

Here is one of the numerous examples of the application of this "theory." It is said that before the imperialist war the parties of the Second International threatened to declare "war against war" if the imperialists should start a war. It is said that on the very eve of the war these parties pigeonholed the "War against war" slogan and applied an opposite one, viz., "War for the imperialist fatherland." It is said that as a result of this change of slogans millions of workers were sent to their death. But it would be a mistake to think that there were some people to blame for this, that someone was unfaithful to the working class or betrayed it. Not at all! Everything happened as it should have happened. Firstly, because the International, it seems, is "an instrument of peace," and not of war. Secondly, because, in view of the "level of the productive forces" which then prevailed, nothing else could be done. The "productive forces" are "to blame." That is the precise explanation vouchsafed to "us" by Mr. Kautsky's "theory of the productive forces." And whoever does not believe in that "theory" is not a Marxist. The role of the parties? Their importance for the movement? But what can a party do against so decisive a factor as the "level of the productive forces"?...

One could cite a host of similar examples of the falsification of Marxism.

It scarcely needs proof that this spurious "Marxism," designed to hide the nakedness of opportunism, is merely a European variety of the selfsame theory of "khvostism" which Lenin fought even before the first Russian revolution.

It scarcely needs proof that the demolition of this theoretical falsification is a preliminary condition for the creation of truly revolutionary parties in the West.

3) *The theory of the proletarian revolution*. Lenin's theory of the proletarian revolution proceeds from three fundamental theses.

First thesis: The domination of finance capital in the advanced capitalist countries; the issue of stocks and bonds as one of the principal operations of finance capital; the export of capital to the sources of raw materials, which is one of the foundations of imperialism; the omnipotence of a financial oligarchy, which is the result of the domination of finance capital – all this reveals the grossly parasitic character of monopolistic capitalism, makes the yoke of the capitalist trusts and syndicates a hundred times more burdensome, intensifies the indignation of the working class with the foundations of capitalism, and brings the masses to the proletarian revolution as their only salvation (see Lenin, *Imperialism*[11]).

Hence the first conclusion: intensification of the revolutionary crisis within the capitalist countries and growth of the elements of an explosion on the internal, proletarian front in the "metropolises."

Second thesis: The increase in the export of capital to the colonies and dependent countries; the expansion of "spheres of influence" and colonial possessions until they cover the whole globe; the transformation of capitalism into a world system of financial enslavement and colonial oppression of the vast majority of the population of the world by a handful of "advanced" countries – all this has, on the one hand, converted the separate national economies and national territories into links in a single chain called world economy, and, on the other hand, split the population of the globe into two camps: a handful of "advanced" capitalist countries which exploit and oppress vast colonies and dependencies, and the huge majority consisting of colonial and dependent countries which are compelled to wage a struggle for liberation from the imperialist yoke (see *Imperialism*).

Hence the second conclusion: intensification of the revolutionary crisis in the colonial countries and growth of the elements of revolt against imperialism on the external, colonial front.

Third thesis: The monopolistic possession of "spheres of influence" and colonies; the uneven development of the capitalist countries, leading to a frenzied struggle for the redivision of the world between the countries which have already seized territories and those claiming their "share"; imperialist wars as the only means of restoring the disturbed "equilibrium" – all this leads to the intensification of the struggle on the third front, the inter-capitalist front, which weakens imperialism and facilitates the union of the first two fronts against imperialism: the front of the revolutionary proletariat and the front of colonial emancipation (see *Imperialism*).

Hence the third conclusion: that under imperialism wars cannot be averted, and that a coalition between the proletarian revolution in Europe and the colonial revolution in the East in a united world front of revolution against the world front of imperialism is inevitable.

Lenin combines all these conclusions into one general conclusion that *"imperialism is the eve of the socialist revolution"* [my italics. – *J. St.*] (see Vol. XIX, p. 71).[*]

The very approach to the question of the proletarian revolution, of the character of the revolution, of its scope, of its depth, the scheme of the revolution in general, changes accordingly.

Formerly, the analysis of the pre-requisites for the proletarian revolution was usually approached from the point of view of the economic state of individual countries. Now, this approach is no longer adequate. Now the matter must be approached from the point of view of the economic state of all or the majority of countries, from the point of view of the state of world economy; for individual countries and individual national economies have ceased to be self-sufficient units, have become links in a single chain called world economy; for the old "cultured" capitalism has evolved into imperialism, and imperialism is a world system of financial enslavement and colonial oppression of the vast majority of the population of the world by a handful of "advanced" countries.

Formerly it was the accepted thing to speak of the existence or absence of objective conditions for the proletarian revolution in individual countries, or, to be more precise, in one or another developed country. Now this point of view is no longer adequate. Now we must speak of the existence of objective conditions for the revolution in the entire system of world imperialist economy as an integral whole; the existence within this system

***

[*] "Preface to Imperialism, the Highest Stage of Capitalism," April 1917.

25

of some countries that are not sufficiently developed industrially cannot serve as an insuperable obstacle to the revolution, *if* the system as a whole or, more correctly, *because* the system as a whole is already ripe for revolution.

Formerly, it was the accepted thing to speak of the proletarian revolution in one or another developed country as of a separate and self-sufficient entity opposing a separate national front of capital as its antipode. Now, this point of view is no longer adequate. Now we must speak of the world proletarian revolution; for the separate national fronts of capital have become links in a single chain called the world front of imperialism, which must be opposed by a common front of the revolutionary movement in all countries.

Formerly the proletarian revolution was regarded exclusively as the result of the internal development of a given country. Now, this point of view is no longer adequate. Now the proletarian revolution must be regarded primarily as the result of the development of the contradictions within the world system of imperialism, as the result of the breaking of the chain of the world imperialist front in one country or another.

Where will the revolution begin? Where, in what country, can the front of capital be pierced first?

Where industry is more developed, where the proletariat constitutes the majority, where there is more culture, where there is more democracy – that was the reply usually given formerly.

No, objects the Leninist theory of revolution, *not necessarily where industry is more developed*, and so forth. The front of capital will be pierced where the chain of imperialism is weakest, for the proletarian revolution is the result of the breaking of the chain of the world imperialist front at its weakest link; and it may turn out that the country which has started the revolution, which has made a breach in the front of capital, is less developed in a capitalist sense than other, more developed, countries, which have, however, remained within the framework of capitalism.

In 1917 the chain of the imperialist world front proved to be weaker in Russia than in the other countries. It was there that the chain broke and provided an outlet for the proletarian revolution. Why? Because in Russian a great popular revolution was unfolding and at its head marched the revolutionary proletariat, which had such an important ally as the vast mass of the peasantry, which was oppressed and exploited by the landlords. Because the revolution there was opposed by such a hideous representative of imperialism as tsarism, which lacked all moral prestige and was deservedly hated by the whole population. The chain proved to be weaker in Russia, although Russia was less developed in a capitalist sense than, say, France or Germany, Britain or America.

Where will the chain break in the near future? Again, where it is weakest. It is not precluded that the chain may break, say, in India. Why? Because that country has a young, militant, revolutionary proletariat, which has such an ally as the national liberation movement – an undoubtedly powerful and undoubtedly important ally. Because there the revolution is confronted by such a well-known foe as foreign imperialism, which has no moral credit and is deservedly hated by all the oppressed and exploited masses in India.

It is also quite possible that the chain will break in Germany. Why? Because the factors which are operating, say, in India are beginning to operate in Germany as well; but, of course, the enormous difference in the level of development between India and Germany cannot but stamp its imprint on the progress and outcome of a revolution in Germany.

That is why Lenin said:

"The West-European capitalist countries will consummate their development toward socialism... not by the even 'maturing' of socialism in them, but by the exploitation of some countries by others, by the exploitation of the first of the countries to be vanquished in the imperialist war combined with the exploitation of the whole of the East. On the other hand, precisely as a result of the first imperialist war, the East has definitely come into revolutionary movement, has been definitely drawn into the general maelstrom of the world revolutionary movement" (see Vol. XXVII, pp. 415-16).[*]

Briefly: the chain of the imperialist front must, as a rule, break where the links are weaker and, at all events, not necessarily where capitalism is more developed, where there is such and such a percentage of proletarians and such and such a percentage of peasants, and so on.

That is why in deciding the question of proletarian revolution statistical estimates of the percentage of the proletarian population in a given country lose the exceptional importance so eagerly attached to them by the doctrinaires of the Second International, who have not understood imperialism and who fear revolution like the plague.

To proceed. The heroes of the Second International asserted (and continue to assert) that between the bourgeois-democratic revolution and the proletarian revolution there is a chasm, or at any rate a Chinese Wall, separating one from the other by a more or less protracted interval of time, during which the bourgeoisie, having come into power, develops capitalism, while the proletariat accumulates strength and prepares for the "decisive struggle" against capitalism. This interval is usually calculated to extend over many decades, if not longer. It scarcely needs proof that this Chinese Wall "theory" is totally devoid of scientific meaning under the conditions of imperialism, that it is and can be only a means of concealing and camouflaging the counter-revolutionary aspirations of the bourgeoisie. It scarcely needs proof that under the conditions of imperialism, fraught as it is with collisions and wars; under the

---

[*] "Better Fewer, But Better," March 1923.

conditions of the "eve of the socialist revolution," when "flour-ishing" capitalism becomes "moribund" capitalism (*Lenin*) and the revolutionary movement is growing in all countries of the world; when imperialism is allying itself with all reactionary forces without exception, down to and including tsarism and serfdom, thus making imperative the coalition of all revolutionary forces, from the proletarian movement of the West, to the national liberation movement of the East; when the overthrow of the survivals of the regime of feudal serfdom becomes impossible without a revolutionary struggle against imperialism – it scarcely needs proof that the bourgeois-democratic revolution, in a more or less developed country, must under such circumstances verge upon the proletarian revolution, that the former must pass into the latter. The history of the revolution in Russia has provided palpable proof that this thesis is correct and incontrovertible. It was not without reason that Lenin, as far back as 1905, on the eve of the first Russian revolution, in his pamphlet *Two Tactics* depicted the bourgeois-democratic revolution and the socialist revolution as two links in the same chain, as a single and integral picture of the sweep of the Russian revolution:

"The proletariat must carry to completion the democratic revolution, by allying to itself the mass of the peasantry in order to crush by force the resistance of the autocracy and to paralyse the instability of the bourgeoisie. The proletariat must accomplish the socialist revolution, by allying to itself the mass of the semi-proletarian elements of the population in order to crush by force the resistance of the bourgeoisie and to paralyse the instability of the peasantry and the petty bourgeoisie. Such are the tasks of the proletariat, which the new Iskraists present so narrowly in all their arguments and resolutions about the sweep of the revolution" (see Lenin, Vol. VIII, p. 96).

There is no need to mention other, later works of Lenin's, in which the idea of the bourgeoisie revolution passing into the proletarian revolution stands out in greater relief than in *Two*

Tactics as one of the cornerstones of the Leninist theory of revolution.

Some comrades believe, it seems, that Lenin arrived at this idea only in 1916, that up to that time he had thought that the revolution in Russia would remain within the bourgeois framework, that power, consequently, would pass from the hands of the organ of the dictatorship of the proletariat and peasantry into the hands of the bourgeoisie and not of the proletariat. It is said that this assertion has even penetrated into our communist press. I must say that this assertion is absolutely wrong, that it is totally at variance with the facts.

I might refer to Lenin's well-known speech at the Third Congress of the Party (1905), in which he defined the dictatorship of the proletariat and peasantry, i.e., the victory of the democratic revolution, not as the "organisation of 'order' " but as the "organisation of war" (see Vol. VII, p. 264).[*]

Further, I might refer to Lenin's well-known articles "On a Provisional Government" (1905),[12] where, outlining the prospects of the unfolding Russian revolution, he assigns to the Party the task of "ensuring that the Russian revolution is not a movement of a few months, but a movement of many years, that it leads, not merely to slight concessions on the part of the powers that be, but to the complete overthrow of those powers"; where, enlarging further on these prospects and linking them with the revolution in Europe, he goes on to say:

"And if we succeed in doing that, then... then the revolutionary conflagration will spread all over Europe; the European worker, languishing under bourgeois reaction, will rise in his turn and will show us 'how it is done'; then the revolutionary wave in Europe will sweep back again into Russia and will convert an epoch of a few revolution-

---

[*] *The Third Congress of the R.S.D.L.P., April 25-May 10, 1905.* "13. Report on the Question of the Participation of the Social-Democrats in a Provisional Revolutionary Government."

ary years into an epoch of several revolutionary decades...." (*ibid.*, p. 191).

I might further refer to a well-known article by Lenin published in November 1915, in which he writes:

"The proletariat is fighting, and will fight valiantly, to capture power, for a republic, for the confiscation of the land... for the participation of the 'non-proletarian masses of the people' in liberating *bourgeois* Russia from *military-feudal* 'imperialism' (= tsarism). And the proletariat will *immediately* [my italics – *J. St.*] take advantage of this liberation of bourgeois Russia from tsarism, from the agrarian power of the landlords, not to aid the rich peasants in their struggle against the rural worker, but to bring about the socialist revolution in alliance with the proletarians of Europe" (see Vol. XVIII, p. 318).[*]

Finally, I might refer to the well-known passage in Lenin's pamphlet *The Proletarian Revolution and the Renegade Kautsky*, where, referring to the above-quoted passage in *Two Tactics* on the sweep of the Russian revolution, he arrives at the following conclusion:

"Things turned out just as we said they would. The course taken by the revolution confirmed the correctness of our reasoning. *First*, with the 'whole' of the peasantry against the monarchy, against the landlords, against the medieval regime (and to that extent the revolution remains bourgeois, bourgeois-democratic). *Then*, with the poor peasants, with the semi-proletarians, with all the exploited, *against capitalism*, including the rural rich, the kulaks, the profiteers, and to that extent the revolution becomes a *socialist* one. To attempt to raise an artificial Chinese Wall between the first and second, to separate them by anything else *than* the degree of preparedness of the proletariat and the degree of its unity with the poor peasants, means monstrously to distort Marxism, to vulgarise it, to replace it by liberalism" (see Vol. XXIII, p. 391).

That is sufficient, I think.

---

[*] "Two Lines of the Revolution."

Very well, we may be told; but if that is the case, why did Lenin combat the idea of "permanent (uninterrupted) revolution"?

Because Lenin proposed that the revolutionary capacities of the peasantry be "exhausted" and that the fullest use be made of their revolutionary energy for the complete liquidation of tsarism and for the transition to the proletarian revolution, whereas the adherents of "permanent revolution" did not understand the important role of the peasantry in the Russian revolution, underestimated the strength of the revolutionary energy of the peasantry, underestimated the strength and ability of the Russian proletariat to lead the peasantry and thereby hampered the work of emancipating the peasantry from the influence of the bourgeois, the work of rallying the peasantry around the proletariat.

Because Lenin proposed that the revolution *be crowned* with the transfer of power to the proletariat, whereas the adherents of "permanent" revolution wanted *to begin* at once with the establishment of the power of the proletariat, failing to realise that in so doing they were closing their eyes to such a "minor detail" as the survivals of serfdom and were leaving out of account so important a force as the Russian peasantry, failing to understand that such a policy could only retard the winning of the peasantry over to the side of the proletariat.

Consequently, Lenin fought the adherents of "permanent" revolution, not over the question of uninterruptedness, for Lenin himself maintained the point of view of uninterrupted revolution, but because they underestimated the role of the peasantry, which is an enormous reserve of the proletariat, because they failed to understand the idea of the hegemony of the proletariat.

The idea of "permanent" revolution should not be regarded as a new idea. It was first advanced by Marx at the end of the forties in his well-known *Address to the Communist League*

(1850). It is from this document that our "permanentists" took the idea of uninterrupted revolution. It should be noted that in taking it from Marx our "permanentists" altered it somewhat, and in altering it "spoilt" it and made it unfit for practical use. The experienced hand of Lenin was needed to rectify this mistake, to take Marx's idea of uninterrupted revolution in its pure form and make it a cornerstone of his theory of revolution.

Here is what Marx says in his *Address* about uninterrupted (permanent) revolution, after enumerating a number of revolutionary-democratic demands which he calls upon the Communists to win:

"While the democratic petty bourgeois wish to bring the revolution to a conclusion as quickly as possible, and with the achievement, at most, of the above demands, it is our interest and our task to make the revolution permanent, until all more or less possessing classes have been forced out of their position of dominance, until the proletariat has conquered state power, and the association of proletarians, not only in one country but in all the dominant countries of the world, has advanced so far that competition among the proletarians of these countries has ceased and that at least the decisive productive forces are concentrated in the hands of the proletarians."[13]

In other words:

a) Marx did not at all propose *to begin* the revolution in the Germany of the fifties with the immediate establishment of proletarian power – *contrary* to the plans of our Russian "permanentists."

b) Marx proposed only that the revolution *be crowned* with the establishment of proletarian state power, by hurling, step by step, one section of the bourgeoisie after another from the heights of power, in order, after the attainment of power by the proletariat, to kindle the fire of revolution in every country – and everything that Lenin taught and carried out in the course of our revolution in pursuit of his theory of the proletarian revolution under the conditions of imperialism was *fully in line* with that proposition.

It follows, then, that our Russian "permanentists" have not only underestimated the role of the peasantry in the Russian revolution and the importance of the idea of hegemony of the proletariat, but have altered (for the worse) Marx's idea of "permanent" revolution and made it unfit for practical use.

That is why Lenin ridiculed the theory of our "permanentists," calling it "original" and "fine," and accusing them of refusing to "think why, for ten whole years, life has passed by this fine theory." (Lenin's article was written in 1915, ten years after the appearance of the theory of the "permanentists" in Russia. See Vol. XVIII, p. 317.)[*]

That is why Lenin regarded this theory as a semi-Menshevik theory and said that it "borrows from the Bolsheviks their call for a resolute revolutionary struggle by the proletariat and the conquest of political power by the latter, and from the Mensheviks the 'repudiation' of the role of the peasantry" (see Lenin's article "Two Lines of the Revolution," *ibid.*).

This, then, is the position in regard to Lenin's idea of the bourgeois-democratic revolution passing into the proletarian revolution, of utilising the bourgeois revolution for the "immediate" transition to the proletarian revolution.

To proceed. Formerly, the victory of the revolution in one country was considered impossible, on the assumption that it would require the combined action of the proletarians of all or at least of a majority of the advanced countries to achieve victory over the bourgeoisie. Now this point of view no longer fits in with the facts. Now we must proceed from the possibility of such a victory, for the uneven and spasmodic character of the development of the various capitalist countries under the conditions of imperialism, the development within imperialism of

---

[*] Ibid.

catastrophic contradictions leading to inevitable wars, the growth of the revolutionary movement in all countries of the world – all this leads, not only to the possibility, but also to the necessity of the victory of the proletariat in individual countries. The history of the revolution in Russia is direct proof of this. At the same time, however, it must be borne in mind that the overthrow of the bourgeoisie can be successfully accomplished only when certain absolutely necessary conditions exist, in the absence of which there can be even no question of the proletariat taking power.

Here is what Lenin says about these conditions in his pamphlet "*Left-Wing" Communism:*

"The fundamental law of revolution, which has been confirmed by all revolutions, and particularly by all three Russian revolutions in the twentieth century, is as follow: it is not enough for revolution that the exploited and oppressed masses should understand the impossibility of living in the old way and demand changes; it is essential for revolution that the exploiters should not be able to live and rule in the old way. Only when the '*lower classes' do not want* the old way, and when the 'upper classes' *cannot carry on in the old way*, – only then can revolution triumph. This truth may be expressed in other words: *Revolution is impossible without a nation-wide crisis (affecting both the exploited and the exploiters)* [my italics. – *J. St.*]. It follows that for revolution it is essential, first, that a majority of the workers (or at least a majority of the class conscious, thinking, politically active workers) should fully understand that revolution is necessary and be ready to sacrifice their lives for it; secondly, that the ruling classes should be passing through a governmental crisis, which draws even the most backward masses into politics,... weakens the government and makes it possible for the revolutionaries to overthrow it rapidly" (see Vol. XXV, p, 222).

But the overthrow of the power of the bourgeoisie and establishment of the power of the proletariat in one country does not yet mean that the complete victory of socialism has been ensured. After consolidating its power and leading the peasantry in its wake the proletariat of the victorious country can and must build a socialist society. But does this mean that it will thereby achieve the complete and final victory of socialism, i.e., does it mean that with the forces of only one country it can finally consolidate socialism and fully guarantee that country against intervention and, consequently, also against restoration? No, it does not. For this the victory of the revolution in at least several countries is needed. Therefore, the development and support of the revolution in other countries is an essential task of the victorious revolution. Therefore, the revolution which has been victorious in one country must regard itself not as a self-sufficient entity, but as an aid, as a means for hastening the victory of the proletariat in other countries.

Lenin expressed this thought succinctly when he said that the task of the victorious revolution is to do "the utmost possible in one country *for* the development, support and awakening of the revolution *in all countries*" (see Vol. XXIII, p. 385).[*]

These, in general, are the characteristic features of Lenin's theory of proletarian revolution.

---

[*] "The Proletarian Revolution and the Renegade Kautsky," October-November 1918.

IV

THE DICTATORSHIP OF THE PROLETARIAT

From this theme I take three fundamental questions:

a) the dictatorship of the proletariat as the instrument of the proletarian revolution;

b) the dictatorship of the proletariat as the rule of the proletariat over the bourgeoisie;

c) Soviet power as the state form of the dictatorship of the proletariat.

1) *The dictatorship of the proletariat as the instrument of the proletarian revolution.* The question of the proletarian dictatorship is above all a question of the main content of the proletarian revolution. The proletarian revolution, its movement, its sweep and its achievements acquire flesh and blood only through the dictatorship of the proletariat. The dictatorship of the proletariat is the instrument of the proletarian revolution, its organ, its most important mainstay, brought into being for the purpose of, firstly, crushing the resistance of the overthrown exploiters and consolidating the achievements of the proletarian revolution, and secondly, carrying the revolution to the complete victory of socialism. The revolution can defeat the bourgeoisie, can overthrow its power, even without the dictatorship of the proletariat. But the revolution will be unable to crush the resistance of the bourgeoisie, to maintain its victory and to push forward to the final victory of socialism unless, at a certain stage in its development, it creates a special organ in the form of the dictatorship of the proletariat as its principle mainstay.

"The fundamental question of every revolution is the question of power" (*Lenin*). Does this mean that all that is required is to assume power, to seize it? No, it does not. The seizure of power is only the beginning. For many reasons, the bourgeoisie that is overthrown in one country remains for a long time stronger than the proletariat which has overthrown it. Therefore, the whole point is to retain power, to consolidate it, to make it invincible. What is needed to attain this? To attain this it is necessary to carry out at least three main tasks that confront the dictatorship of the proletariat "on the morrow" of victory:

a) to break the resistance of the landlords and capitalists who have been overthrown and expropriated by the revolution, to liquidate every attempt on their part to restore the power of capital;

b) to organise construction in such a way as to rally all the working people around the proletariat, and to carry on this work along the lines of preparing for the elimination, the abolition of classes;

c) to arm the revolution, to organise the army of the revolution for the struggle against foreign enemies, for the struggle against imperialism.

The dictatorship of the proletariat is needed to carry out, to fulfil these tasks.

"The transition from capitalism to communism," says Lenin, "represents an entire historical epoch. Until this epoch has terminated, the exploiters inevitably cherish the hope of restoration, and this *hope* is converted into *attempts* at restoration. And after their first serious defeat, the overthrown exploiters – who had not expected their overthrow, never believed it possible, never conceded the thought of it – throw themselves with energy grown tenfold, with furious passion and hatred grown a hundredfold, into the battle for the recovery of the 'paradise' of which they have been deprived, on behalf of their families, who had been leading such a sweet and easy life and whom now the 'common herd' is condemning to ruin and destitution (or to 'common' labour...). In the train of the capitalist exploiters follow the broad masses of the petty bourgeoisie, with regard to whom decades of historical experience of all countries testify that they vacillate and hesitate, one day marching behind the proletariat and the next day taking fright at the difficulties of the revolution; that they become panic-stricken at the first defeat or semi-defeat of the workers, grow nervous, rush about, snivel, and run from one camp into the other" (see Vol. XXIII, p. 355).[*]

The bourgeoisie has its grounds for making attempts at restoration, because for a long time after its overthrow it remains stronger than the proletariat which has overthrown it.

"If the exploiters are defeated in one country only" says Lenin, "and this, of course, is the typical case, since a simultaneous revolution in a number of countries is a rare exception, they *still* remain *stronger* than the exploited" (*ibid.*, p. 354).

Wherein lies the strength of the overthrown bourgeoisie?

Firstly, "in the strength of international capital, in the strength and durability of the international connections of the bourgeoisie" (see Vol. XXV, p. 173).[†]

Secondly, in the fact that "for a long time after the revolution the exploiters inevitably retain a number of great practical advantages: they still have money (it is impossible to abolish money all at once); some moveable property – often fairly considerable; they still have various connections, habits of organisation and management, knowledge of all the 'secrets' (customs, methods, means and possibilities) of management, superior education, close connections with the higher technical personnel (who live and think like the bourgeoisie), incomparably greater experience in the art of war (this is very important), and so on, and so forth" (see Vol. XXIII, p. 354).[‡]

Thirdly, "in the *force of habit*, in the strength of *small production*. For, unfortunately, small production is still very, very widespread in the world, and small production *engenders* capitalism and the bourgeoisie continuously, daily, hourly, spontaneously, and on a mass scale"... for "the abolition of classes means only not only driving out the landlords and capitalists – that we accomplished with comparative ease – it also means *abolishing the small commodity producers*, and

---

[*] Ibid.
[†] " 'Left-Wing' Communism, an Infantile Disorder," April-May 1920.
[‡] "The Proletarian Revolution and the Renegade Kautsky."

they *cannot be driven out*, or crushed; we *must live in harmony* with them, they can (and must) be remoulded and re-educated only by very prolonged, slow, cautious organizational work (see Vol. XXV, pp. 173 and 189).*

That is why Lenin says:

"The dictatorship of the proletariat is a most determined and most ruthless war waged by the new class against a *more powerful enemy*, the bourgeoisie, whose resistance is increased *tenfold* by its over-throw,..."

and

"The dictatorship of the proletariat is a stubborn struggle – bloody and bloodless, violent and peaceful, military and economic, educa-tional and administrative – against the forces and traditions of the old society" (*ibid.*, pp. 173 and 190).

It scarcely needs proof that there is not the slightest possi-bility of carrying out these tasks in a short period, of accom-plishing all this in a few years. Therefore, the dictatorship of the proletariat, the transition from capitalism to communism, must not be regarded as a fleeting period of "super-revolutionary" acts and decrees, but as an entire historical era, replete with civil wars and external conflicts, with persistent organisational work and economic construction, with advances and retreats, victories and defeats. The historical era is needed not only to create the economic and cultural prerequisites for the complete victory of socialism, but also to enable the proletariat, firstly, to educate itself and become steeled as a force capable of govern-ing the country, and, secondly, to re-educate and remould the petty-bourgeois strata along such lines as will assure the organi-sation of socialist production.

---

* " 'Left-Wing' Communism, an Infantile Disorder."

"You will have to go through fifteen, twenty, fifty years of civil wars and international conflicts," Marx said to the workers, "not only to change existing conditions, but also to change yourselves and to make yourselves capable of wielding political power" (see K. Marx and F. Engels, *Works*, Vol. VIII, p. 506).[*]

Continuing and developing Marx's idea still further, Lenin wrote that:

"It will be necessary under the dictatorship of the proletariat to re-educate millions of peasants and small proprietors, hundreds of thousands of office employees, officials and bourgeois intellectuals, to subordinate them all to the proletarian state and to proletarian leadership, to overcome their bourgeois habits and traditions," just as we must "– in a protracted struggle waged on the basis of the dictatorship of the proletariat – re-educate the proletarians themselves, who do not abandon their petty-bourgeois prejudices at one stroke, by a miracle, at the bidding of the Virgin Mary, at the bidding of a slogan, resolution or decree, but only in the course of a long and difficult mass struggle against the mass petty-bourgeois influences" (see Vol. XXV, pp. 248 and 247).[†]

2) *The dictatorship of the proletariat as the rule of the proletariat over the bourgeoisie.* From the foregoing it is evident that the dictatorship of the proletariat is not a mere change of personalities in the government, a change of the "cabinet," etc., leaving the old economic and political order intact. The Mensheviks and the opportunists of all countries, who fear dictatorship like fire and in their fright substitute the concept "conquest of power" for the concept of dictatorship, usually reduce the "conquest of power" to a change of the "cabinet," to the accession to power of a new ministry made up of people like Scheidemann and Noske, MacDonald and Henderson. It is hardly necessary to explain that these and similar cabinet changes have

---

[*] "Revelations About the Cologne Communist Trial," October-December 1852.
[†] " 'Left-Wing' Communism, an Infantile Disorder."

41

nothing in common with the dictatorship of the proletariat, with the conquest of real power by the real proletariat. With the MacDonalds and Scheidemanns in power, while the old bourgeois order is allowed to remain, their so-called governments cannot be anything else than an apparatus serving the bourgeoisie, a screen to conceal the ulcers of imperialism, a weapon in the hands of the bourgeoisie against the revolutionary movement of the oppressed and exploited masses. Capital needs such governments as a screen when it finds it inconvenient, unprofitable, difficult to oppress and exploit the masses without the aid of a screen. Of course, the appearance of such governments is a symptom that "over there" (i.e., in the capitalist camp) all is not quite "at the Shipka Pass";[14] nevertheless, governments of this kind inevitably remain governments of capital in disguise. The government of a MacDonald or a Scheidemann is as far removed from the conquest of power by the proletariat as the sky from the earth. The dictatorship of the proletariat is not a change of government, but a new state, with new organs of power, both central and local; it is the state of the proletariat, which has arisen on the ruins of the old state, the state of the bourgeoisie.

The dictatorship of the proletariat arises not on the basis of the bourgeois order, but in the process of the breaking up of this order, after the overthrow of the bourgeoisie, in the process of the expropriation of the landlords and capitalists, in the process of the socialisation of the principal instruments and means of production, in the process of violent proletarian revolution. The dictatorship of the proletariat is a revolutionary power based on the use of force against the bourgeoisie.

The state is a machine in the hands of the ruling class for suppressing the resistance of its class enemies. *In this respect* the dictatorship of the proletariat does not differ essentially from the dictatorship of any other class, for the proletarian state is a machine for the suppression of the bourgeoisie. But there is one *substantial* difference. This difference consists in the fact that all hitherto existing class states have been dictatorships of an exploiting minority over the exploited majority, whereas the dictatorship of the proletariat is the dictatorship of the exploited majority over the exploiting minority.

Briefly: *the dictatorship of the proletariat is the rule – unrestricted by law and based on force – of the proletariat over the bourgeoisie, a rule enjoying the sympathy and support of the labouring and exploited masses* (Lenin, *The State and Revolution*).

From this follow two main conclusions:

First conclusion: The dictatorship of the proletariat cannot be "complete" democracy, democracy for *all*, for the rich as well as for the poor; the dictatorship of the proletariat "must be a state that is democratic *in a new way* (*for* [my italics – *J. St.*] the proletarians and the non-propertied in general) and dictatorial *in a new way* (*against* [my italics – *J. St.*] the bourgeoisie)" (see Vol. XXI, p. 393).* The talk of Kautsky and Co. about universal equality, about "pure" democracy, about "perfect" democracy, and the like, is a bourgeois disguise of the indubitable fact that equality between exploited and exploiters is impossible. The theory of "pure" democracy is the theory of the upper stratum of the working class, which has been broken in and is being fed by the imperialist robbers. It was brought into being for the purpose of concealing the ulcers of capitalism, of embellishing imperialism and lending it moral strength in the struggle against the exploited masses. Under capitalism there are no real "liberties" for the exploited, nor can there be, if for no other reason than that the premises, printing plants, paper supplies, etc., indispensable for the enjoyment of "liberties" are the privilege of the exploiters. Under capitalism the exploited masses do not, nor can they ever, really participate in governing the coun-

---

* "The State and Revolution," August-September 1917.

try, if for no other reason than that, even under the most democratic regime, under conditions of capitalism, governments are not set up by the people but by the Rothschilds and Stinneses, the Rockefellers and Morgans. Democracy under capitalism is *capitalist* democracy, the democracy of the exploiting minority, based on the restriction of the rights of the exploited majority and directed against this majority. Only under the proletarian dictatorship are real liberties for the exploited and real participation of the proletarians and peasants in governing the country possible. Under the dictatorship of the proletariat, democracy is *proletarian* democracy, the democracy of the exploited majority, based on the restriction of the rights of the exploiting minority and directed against this minority.

Second conclusion: The dictatorship of the proletariat cannot arise as the result of the peaceful development of bourgeois society and of bourgeois democracy; it can arise only as the result of the smashing of the bourgeois state machine, the bourgeois army, the bourgeois bureaucratic apparatus, the bourgeois police.

"...The working class cannot simply lay hold of the ready-made state machinery, and wield it for its own purposes," say Marx and Engels in a preface to the *Communist Manifesto*. The task of the proletarian revolution is "no longer, as before, to transfer the bureaucratic-military machine from one hand to another, *but to smash* it and this is the preliminary condition for every real people's revolution on the continent," says Marx in his letter to Kugelmann in 1871.[15]

Marx's qualifying phrases about the continent gave the opportunists and Mensheviks of all countries a pretext for clamouring that Marx had thus conceded the possibility of the peaceful evolution of bourgeois democracy into a proletarian democracy, at least in certain countries outside the European continent (Britain, America). Marx did in fact concede that possibility, and he had good grounds for conceding it in regard to Britain and America in the seventies of the last century, when monopoly capitalism and imperialism did not yet exist, and when these countries, owing to the particular conditions of their development, had as much as yet no developed militarism and bureaucracy. That was the situation before the appearance of developed imperialism. But later, after a lapse of thirty or forty years, when the situation in these countries had radically changed, when imperialism had developed and had embraced all capitalist countries without exception, when militarism and bureaucracy had appeared in Britain and America also, when the particular conditions for peaceful development in Britain and America had disappeared – then the qualification in regard to these countries necessarily could no longer hold good.

"Today," said Lenin, "in 1917, in the epoch of the first great imperialist war, this qualification made by Marx is no longer valid. Both Britain and America, the biggest and the last representatives – in the whole world – of Anglo-Saxon 'liberty' in the sense that they had no militarism and bureaucracy, have completely sunk into the all-European filthy, bloody morass of bureaucratic-military institutions which subordinate everything to themselves and trample everything underfoot. Today, in Britain and in America, too, 'the preliminary condition for every real people's revolution' is the *smashing*, the *destruction* of the 'ready-made state machinery' (perfected in those countries, between 1914 and 1917, up to the 'European' general imperialist standard)" (see Vol. XXI, p. 395).[*]

In other words, the law of violent proletarian revolution, the law of the smashing of the bourgeois state machine as a preliminary condition for such a revolution, is an inevitable law of the revolutionary movement in the imperialist countries of the world.

Of course, in the remote future, if the proletariat is victorious in the principal capitalist countries, and if the present capitalist encirclement is replaced by a socialist encirclement, a "peaceful" path of development is quite possible for certain

---

[*] Ibid.

capitalist countries, whose capitalists, in view of the "unfavourable" international situation, will consider it expedient "voluntarily" to make substantial concessions to the proletariat. But this supposition applies only to a remote and possible future. With regard to the immediate future, there is no ground whatsoever for this supposition.

Therefore, Lenin is right in saying:

"The proletarian revolution is impossible without the forcible destruction of the bourgeois state machine and the substitution for it of a *new one*" (see Vol. XXIII, p. 342).[*]

3) *Soviet power as the state form of the dictatorship of the proletariat.* The victory of the dictatorship of the proletariat signifies the suppression of the bourgeoisie, the smashing of the bourgeois state machine and the substitution of proletarian democracy for bourgeois democracy. That is clear. But by means of what organisation can this colossal work be carried out? The old forms of organisation of the proletariat, which grew up on the basis of bourgeois parliamentarism, are inadequate for this work – of that there can hardly be any doubt. What, then, are the new forms of organisation of the proletariat that are capable of serving as the gravediggers of the bourgeois state machine, that are capable not only of smashing this machine, not only of substituting proletarian democracy for bourgeois democracy, but also of becoming the foundation of the proletarian state power?

This new form of organisation of the proletariat is the Soviets.

Wherein lies the strength of the Soviets as compared with the old forms of organisation?

---

[*] "The Proletarian Revolution and the Renegade Kautsky."

In that the Soviets are the most *all-embracing* mass organisations of the proletariat, for they and they alone embrace all workers without exception.

In that the Soviets are the *only* mass organisations which unite all the oppressed and exploited, workers and peasants, soldiers and sailors, and in which the vanguard of the masses, the proletariat, can, for this reason, most easily and most completely exercise its political leadership of the mass struggle.

In that the Soviets are the *most powerful organs* of the revolutionary struggle of the masses, of the political actions of the masses, of the uprising of the masses – organs capable of breaking the omnipotence of finance capital and its political appendages.

In that the Soviets are the *immediate* organisations of the masses themselves, i.e., they are the *most democratic* and therefore the most authoritative organisations of the masses, which facilitate to the utmost their participation in the work of building up the new state and in its administration, and which bring into full play the revolutionary energy, initiative and creative abilities of the masses in the struggle for the destruction of the old order, in the struggle for the new, proletarian order.

Soviet power is the union and constitution of the local Soviets into one common state organisation, into the state organisation of the proletariat as the vanguard of the oppressed and exploited masses and as the ruling class – their union in the Republic of the Soviets.

The essence of Soviet power consists in the fact that these most all-embracing and most revolutionary mass organisations of precisely those classes that were oppressed by the capitalists and landlords are now the "*permanent and sole* basis of the whole power of the state, of the whole state apparatus"; that "precisely those masses which even in the most democratic bourgeois republics," while being equal in law, "have in fact been prevented by thousands of tricks and devices from taking part in political life and from enjoying democratic rights and liberties, are now drawn unfailingly into *constant* and, moreover, *decisive* participation in the democratic administration of the state" [all italics mine – *J. St.*] (see Lenin, Vol. XXIV, p. 13).*

That is why Soviet power is a *new form* of state organisation, different in principle from the old bourgeois-democratic and parliamentary form, a *new type* of state, adapted not to the task of exploiting and oppressing the labouring masses, but to the task of completely emancipating them from all oppression and exploitation, to the tasks facing the dictatorship of the proletariat.

Lenin is right in saying that with the appearance of Soviet power "the era of bourgeois-democratic parliamentarism has drawn to a close and a new chapter in world history – the era of proletarian dictatorship – has been opened."

Wherein lie the characteristic features of Soviet power?

In that Soviet power is the most all-embracing and most democratic state organisation of all possible state organisations while classes continue to exist; for, being the arena of the bond and collaboration between the workers and the exploited peasants in their struggle against the exploiters, and basing itself in its work on this bond and on this collaboration, Soviet power is thus the power of the majority of the population over the minority, it is the state of the majority, the expression of its dictatorship.

In that Soviet power is the most internationalist of all state organisations in class society, for, by destroying every kind of national oppression and resting on the collaboration of the la-

---

* *First Congress of the Communist International, March 2-6, 1919.* "2. Theses and Report on Bourgeois Democracy and the Dictatorship of the Proletariat."

bouring masses of the various nationalities, it facilitates the uniting of these masses into a single state union.

In that Soviet power, by its very structure, facilitates the task of leading the oppressed and exploited masses by the vanguard of these masses – by the proletariat, as the most united and most politically conscious core of the Soviets.

"The experience of all revolutions and of all movements of the oppressed classes, the experience of the world socialist movement teaches us," says Lenin, "that the proletariat alone is able to unite and lead the scattered and backward strata of the toiling and exploited population" (see Vol. XXIV, p. 14).[*] The point is that the structure of Soviet power facilitates the practical application of the lessons drawn from this experience.

In that Soviet power, by combining legislative and executive power in a single state organisation and replacing territorial electoral constituencies by industrial units, factories and mills, thereby directly links the workers and the labouring masses in general with the apparatus of state administration, teaches them how to govern the country.

In that Soviet power alone is capable of releasing the army from its subordination to bourgeois command and of converting it from the instrument of oppression of the people which it is under the bourgeois order into an instrument for the liberation of the people from the yoke of the bourgeoisie, both native and foreign.

In that "the Soviet organisation of the state alone is capable of immediately and effectively smashing and finally destroying the old, i.e., the bourgeois, bureaucratic and judicial apparatus" (*ibid*).

In that the Soviet form of state alone, by drawing the mass organisations of the toilers and exploited into constant and unrestricted participation in state administration, is capable of

---

[*] Ibid.

preparing the ground for the withering away of the state, which is one of the basic elements of the future stateless communist society.

The Republic of Soviets is thus the political form, so long sought and finally discovered, within the framework of which the economic emancipation of the proletariat, the complete victory of socialism, must be accomplished.

The Paris Commune was the embryo of this form; Soviet power is its development and culmination.

That is why Lenin says:

"The Republic of Soviets of Workers', Soldiers', and Peasants' Deputies is not only the form of a higher type of democratic institution..., but is the *only* [my italics – *J. St.*] form capable of ensuring the most painless transition to socialism" (see Vol. XXII, p. 131).[*]

---

[*] "Theses on the Constituent Assembly," December 1917.

V

THE PEASANT QUESTION

From this theme I take four questions:

a) the presentation of the question;

b) the peasantry during the bourgeois-democratic revolution;

c) the peasantry during the proletarian revolution;

d) the peasantry after the consolidation of Soviet power.

1) *The presentation of the question.* Some think that the fundamental thing in Leninism is the peasant question, that the point of departure of Leninism is the question of the peasantry, of its role, its relative importance. This is absolutely wrong. The fundamental question of Leninism, its point of departure, is not the peasant question, but the question of the dictatorship of the proletariat, of the conditions under which it can be achieved, of the conditions under which it can be consolidated. The peasant question, as the question of the ally of the proletariat in its struggle for power, is a derivative question.

This circumstance, however, does not in the least deprive the peasant question of the serious and vital importance it unquestionably has for the proletarian revolution. It is known that the serious study of the peasant question in the ranks of Russian Marxists began precisely on the eve of the first revolution (1905), when the question of overthrowing tsarism and of realising the hegemony of the proletariat confronted the Party in all its magnitude, and when the question of the ally of the proletariat in the impending bourgeois revolution became of vital importance. It is also known that the peasant question in Russia assumed a still more urgent character during the proletarian revolution, when the question of the dictatorship of the proletariat, of achieving and maintaining it, led to the question of allies for the proletariat in the impending proletarian revolution. And this was natural. Those who are marching towards and preparing to assume power cannot but be interested in the question of who are their real allies.

In this sense the peasant question is part of the general question of the dictatorship of the proletariat, and as such it is one of the most vital problems of Leninism.

The attitude of indifference and sometimes even of outright aversion displayed by the parties of the Second International towards the peasant question is to be explained not only by the specific conditions of development in the West. It is to be explained primarily by the fact that these parties do not believe in the proletarian dictatorship, that they fear revolution and have no intention of leading the proletariat to power. And those who are afraid of revolution, who do not intend to lead the proletarians to power, cannot be interested in the question of allies for the proletariat in the revolution – to them the question of allies is one of indifference, of no immediate significance. The ironical attitude of the heroes of the Second International towards the peasant question is regarded by them as a sign of good breeding, a sign of "true" Marxism. As a matter of fact, there is not a grain of Marxism in this, for indifference towards so important a question as the peasant question on the eve of the proletarian revolution is the reverse side of the repudiation of the dictatorship of the proletariat, it is an unmistakable sign of downright betrayal of Marxism.

The question is as follows: Are the revolutionary potentialities latent in the peasantry by virtue of certain conditions of its existence *already exhausted,* or not; and if not, *is there any hope, any basis,* for utilising these potentialities for the proletarian revolution, for transforming the peasantry, the exploited majority of it, from the reserve of the bourgeoisie which it was during the bourgeois revolutions in the West and still is even now, into a reserve of the proletariat, into its ally?

Leninism replies to this question in the affirmative, i.e., it recognises the existence of revolutionary capacities in the ranks of the majority of the peasantry, and the possibility of using these in the interests of the proletarian dictatorship.

The history of the three revolutions in Russia fully corroborates the conclusion of Leninism on this score.

Hence the practical conclusion that the toiling masses of the peasantry must be supported in their struggle against bondage and exploitation, in their struggle for deliverance from oppression and poverty. This does not mean, of course, that the proletariat must support *every* peasant movement. What we have in mind here is support for a movement or struggle of the peasantry which, directly or indirectly, facilitates the emancipation movement of the proletariat, which, in one way or another, brings grist to the mill of the proletarian revolution, and which helps to transform the peasantry into a reserve and ally of the working class.

2) *The peasantry during the bourgeois-democratic revolution.* This period extends from the first Russian revolution (1905) to the second revolution (February 1917), inclusive. The characteristic feature of this period is the emancipation of the peasantry from the influence of the liberal bourgeoisie, the peasantry's *desertion* of the Cadets, its *turn* towards the proletariat, towards the Bolshevik Party. The history of this period is the history of the struggle between the Cadets (the liberal bourgeoisie) and the Bolsheviks (the proletariat) for the peasantry. The outcome of this struggle was decided by the Duma period, for the period of the four Dumas served as an object lesson to the peasantry, and this lesson brought home to the peasantry the fact that they would receive neither land nor liberty at the hands of the Cadets; that the tsar was wholly in favour of the landlords, and that the Cadets were supporting the tsar; that the only

force they could rely on for assistance was the urban workers, the proletariat. The imperialist war merely confirmed the lessons of the Duma period and consummated the peasantry's desertion of the bourgeoisie, consummated the isolation of the liberal bourgeoisie; for the years of the war revealed the utter futility, the utter deceptiveness of all hopes of obtaining peace from the tsar and his bourgeois allies. Without the object lessons of the Duma period, the hegemony of the proletariat would have been impossible.

That is how the alliance between the workers and the peasants in the bourgeois-democratic revolution took shape. That is how the hegemony (leadership) of the proletariat in the common struggle for the overthrow of tsarism took shape – the hegemony which led to the February Revolution of 1917.

The bourgeois revolutions in the West (Britain, France, Germany, Austria) took, as is well known, a different road. There, hegemony in the revolution belonged not to the proletariat, which by reason of its weakness did not and could not represent an independent political force, but to the liberal bourgeoisie. There the peasantry obtained its emancipation from feudal regimes, not at the hands of the proletariat, which was numerically weak and unorganised, but at the hands of the bourgeoisie. There the peasantry marched against the old order side by side with the liberal bourgeoisie. There the peasantry acted as the reserve of the bourgeoisie. There the revolution, in consequences of this, led to an enormous increase in the political weight of the bourgeoisie.

In Russia, on the contrary, the bourgeois revolution produced quite opposite results. The revolution in Russia led not to the strengthening, but to the weakening of the bourgeoisie as a political force, not to an increase in its political reserves, but to the loss of its main reserve, to the loss of the peasantry. The bourgeois revolution in Russia brought to the forefront not the liberal bourgeoisie but the revolutionary proletariat, rallying around the latter the millions of the peasantry.

Incidentally, this explains why the bourgeois revolution in Russia passed into a proletarian revolution in a comparatively short space of time. The hegemony of the proletariat was the embryo of, and the transitional stage to, the dictatorship of the proletariat.

How is this peculiar phenomenon of the Russian revolution, which has no precedent in the history of the bourgeois revolutions of the West, to be explained? Whence this peculiarity?

It is to be explained by the fact that the bourgeois revolution unfolded in Russia under more advanced conditions of class struggle than in the West; that the Russian proletariat had at that time already become an independent political force, whereas the liberal bourgeoisie, frightened by the revolutionary spirit of the proletariat, lost all semblance of revolutionary spirit (especially after the lessons of 1905) and turned towards an alliance with the tsar and the landlords against the revolution, against the workers and peasants.

We should bear in mind the following circumstances, which determined the peculiar character of the Russian bourgeois revolution.

a) The unprecedented concentration of Russia industry on the eve of the revolution. It is known, for instance, that in Russia 54 per cent of all the workers were employed in enterprises employing over 500 workers each, whereas in so highly developed a country as the United States of America no more than 33 per cent of all the workers were employed in such enterprises. It scarcely needs proof that this circumstance alone, in view of the existence of a revolutionary party like the Party of the Bolsheviks, transformed the working class of Russia into an immense force in the political life of the country.

b) The hideous forms of exploitation in the factories, coupled with the intolerable police regime of the tsarist henchmen

– a circumstance which transformed every important strike of the workers into an imposing political action and steeled the working class as a force that was revolutionary to the end.

c) The political flabbiness of the Russian bourgeoisie, which after the Revolution of 1905 turned into servility to tsarism and downright counter-revolution – a fact to be explained not only by the revolutionary spirit of the Russian proletariat, which flung the Russian bourgeoisie into the embrace of tsarism, but also by the direct dependence of this bourgeoisie upon government contracts.

d) The existence in the countryside of the most hideous and most intolerable survivals of serfdom, coupled with the unlimited power of the landlords – a circumstance which threw the peasantry into the embrace of the revolution.

e) Tsarism, which stifled everything that was alive, and whose tyranny aggravated the oppression of the capitalist and the landlord – a circumstance which united the struggle of the workers and peasants into a single torrent of revolution.

f) The imperialist war, which fused all these contradictions in the political life of Russia into a profound revolutionary crisis, and which lent the revolution tremendous striking force.

To whom could the peasantry turn under these circumstances? From whom could it seek support against the unlimited power of the landlords, against the tyranny of the tsar, against the devastating war which was ruining it? From the liberal bourgeoisie? But it was an enemy, as the long years of experience of all four Dumas had proved. From the Socialist-Revolutionaries? The Socialist-Revolutionaries were "better" than the Cadets, of course, and their programme was "suitable," almost a peasant programme; but what could the Socialist-Revolutionaries offer, considering that they thought of relying only on the peasants and were weak in the towns, from which the enemy primarily drew its forces? Where was the new force which would stop at nothing either in town or country, which would boldly march in the front ranks to fight the tsar and the landlords, which would help the peasantry to extricate itself from bondage, from land hunger, from oppression, from war? Was there such a force in Russia at all? Yes, there was. It was the Russian proletariat, which had shown its strength, its ability to fight to the end, its boldness and revolutionary spirit, as far back as 1905.

At any rate, there was no other such force; nor could any other be found anywhere.

That is why the peasantry, when it turned its back on the Cadets and attached itself to the Socialist-Revolutionaries, at the same time came to realise the necessity of submitting to the leadership of such a courageous leader of the revolution as the Russian proletariat.

Such were the circumstances which determined the peculiar character of the Russian bourgeois revolution.

3) *The peasantry during the proletarian revolution.* This period extends from the February Revolution of 1917 to the October Revolution of 1917. This period is comparatively short, eight months in all; but from the point of view of the political enlightenment and revolutionary training of the masses these eight months can safely be put on a par with whole decades of ordinary constitutional development, for they were eight months of *revolution.* The characteristic feature of this period was the further revolutionisation of the peasantry, its disillusionment with the Socialist-Revolutionaries, the peasantry's *desertion* of the Socialist-Revolutionaries, its new *turn* toward a direct rally around the proletariat as the only consistently revolutionary force capable of leading the country to peace. The history of this period is the history of the struggle between the Socialist-Revolutionaries (petty-bourgeois democracy) and the Bolsheviks (proletarian democracy) for the peasantry, to win over the majority of the peasantry. The outcome of this struggle was decided by the coalition period, the Kerensky period, the

refusal of the Socialist-Revolutionaries and the Mensheviks to confiscate the landlords' land, the fight of the Socialist-Revolutionaries and Mensheviks to continue the war, the June offensive at the front, the introduction of capital punishment for soldiers, the Kornilov revolt.

Whereas before, in the preceding period, the basic question had been the overthrow of the tsar and of the power of the land-lords, now, in the period following the February Revolution, when there was no longer any tsar, and when the interminable war had exhausted the economy of the country and utterly ru-ined the peasantry, the question of liquidating the war became the main problem of the revolution. The centre of gravity had manifestly shifted from purely internal questions to the main question – the war. "End the war," "Let's get out of the war" – such was the general outcry of the war-weary nation and pri-marily of the peasantry.

But in order to get out of the war it was necessary to over-throw the Provisional Government, it was necessary to over-throw the power of the bourgeoisie, it was necessary to overthrow the power of the Socialist-Revolutionaries and Men-sheviks, for they, and they alone, were dragging out the war to a "victorious finish." Practically, there was no way of getting out of the war except by overthrowing the bourgeoisie.

This was a new revolution, a proletarian revolution, for it ousted from power the last group of the imperialist bourgeoisie, its extreme Left wing, the Socialist-Revolutionary Party and the Mensheviks, in order to set up a new, proletarian power, the power of the Soviets, in order to put in power the party of the revolutionary proletariat, the Bolshevik Party, the party of the revolutionary struggle against the imperialist war and for a de-mocratic peace. The majority of the peasantry supported the struggle of the workers for peace, for the power of the Soviets.

There was no other way out for the peasantry. Nor could there be any other way out.

Thus, the Kerensky period was a great object lesson for the toiling masses of the peasantry, for it showed clearly that with the Socialist-Revolutionaries and Mensheviks in power the country could not extricate itself from the war, and the peasants would never get either land or liberty; that the Mensheviks and Socialist-Revolutionaries differed from the Cadets only in their honeyed phrases and false premises, while they actually pursued the same imperialist, Cadet policy; that the only power that could lead the country on to the proper road was the power of the Soviets. The further prolongation of the war merely confirmed the truth of this lesson, spurred on the revolution, and drove millions of peasants and soldiers to *rally directly* around the proletarian revolution. The isolation of the Socialist-Revolutionaries and Mensheviks became an incontrovertible fact. Without the object lessons of the coalition period the dictatorship of the proletariat would have been impossible.

Such were the circumstances which facilitated the process of the bourgeois revolution passing into the proletarian revolution.

That is how the dictatorship of the proletariat took shape in Russia.

4) *The peasantry after the consolidation of Soviet power.* Whereas before, in the first period of the revolution, the main objective was the overthrow of tsarism, and later, after the February Revolution, the primary objective was to get out of the imperialist war by overthrowing the bourgeoisie, now, after the liquidation of the civil war and the consolidation of Soviet power, questions of economic construction came to the forefront. Strengthen and develop the nationalised industry; for this purpose link up industry with peasant economy through state-regulated trade; replace the surplus-appropriation system by the tax in kind so as, later on, by gradually lowering the tax in kind, to reduce matters to the exchange of products of industry for the products of peasant farming; revive trade and develop the co-

operatives, drawing into them the vast masses of the peasantry – this is how Lenin outlined the immediate tasks of economic construction on the way to building the foundations of socialist economy.

It is said that this task may prove beyond the strength of a peasant country like Russia. Some sceptics even say that it is simply utopian, impossible, for the peasantry is a peasantry – it consists of small producers, and therefore cannot be of use in organising the foundations of socialist production.

But the sceptics are mistaken, for they fail to take into account certain circumstances which in the present case are of decisive significance. Let us examine the most important of these:

Firstly. The peasantry in the Soviet Union must not be confused with the peasantry in the West. A peasantry that has been schooled in three revolutions, that fought against the tsar and the power of the bourgeoisie side by side with the proletariat and under the leadership of the proletariat, a peasantry that has received land and peace at the hands of the proletarian revolution and by reason of this has become the reserve of the proletariat – such a peasantry cannot but be different from a peasantry which during the bourgeois revolution fought under the leadership of the liberal bourgeoisie, which received land at the hands of that bourgeoisie, and in view of this became the reserve of the bourgeoisie. It scarcely needs proof that the Soviet peasantry, which has learnt to appreciate its political friendship and political collaboration with the proletariat and which owes its freedom to this friendship and collaboration, cannot but represent exceptionally favourable material for economic collaboration with the proletariat.

Engels said that "the conquest of political power by the Socialist Party has become a matter of the not too distant future," that "in order to conquer political power this party must first go from the towns to the country, must become a power in the countryside" (see Engels, *The Peasant Question*, 1922 ed.[16]). He wrote this in the nineties of the last century, having in mind the Western peasantry. Does it need proof that the Russian Communists, after accomplishing an enormous amount of work in this field in the course of three revolutions, have already succeeded in gaining in the countryside an influence and backing the like of which our Western comrades dare not even dream of? How can it be denied that this circumstance must decidedly facilitate the organisation of economic collaboration between the working class and the peasantry of Russia?

The sceptics maintain that the small peasants are a factor that is incompatible with socialist construction. But listen to what Engels says about the small peasants of the West:

"We... are decidedly on the side of the small peasant; we shall do everything at all permissible to make his lot more bearable, to facilitate his transition to the co-operative should he decide to do so, and even to make it possible for him to remain on his small holding for a protracted length of time to think the matter over, should he still be unable to bring himself to this decision. We do this not only because we consider the small peasant who does his own work as virtually belonging to us, but also in the direct interest of the Party. The greater the number of peasants whom we can save from being actually hurled down into the proletariat, whom we can win to our side while they are still peasants, the more quickly and easily the social transformation will be accomplished. It will serve us nought to wait with this transformation until capitalist production has developed everywhere to its utmost consequences, until the last small handicraftsman and last small peasant have fallen victim to capitalist large-scale production. The material sacrifices to be made for this purpose in the interest of the peasants and to be defrayed out of public funds can, from the point of view of capitalist economy, be viewed only as money thrown away, but it is nevertheless an excellent investment because it will effect a perhaps tenfold saving in the cost of the social reorganisation in general. In this sense we can, therefore, afford to deal very liberally with the peasants" (*ibid.*).[17]

That is what Engels said, having in mind the Western peasantry. But is it not clear that what Engels said can nowhere be realised so easily and so completely as in the land of the dictatorship of the proletariat? Is it not clear that only in Soviet Russia is it possible at once and to the fullest extent for "the small peasant who does his own work" to come over to our side, for the "material sacrifices" necessary for this to be made, and for the necessary "liberality towards the peasants" to be displayed? Is it not clear that these and similar measures for the benefit of the peasantry are already being carried out in Russia? How can it be denied that this circumstance, in its turn, must facilitate and advance the work of economic construction in the land of the Soviets?

Secondly. Agriculture in Russia must not be confused with agriculture in the West. There, agriculture is developed along the ordinary lines of capitalism, under conditions of profound differentiation among the peasantry, with large landed estates and private capitalist latifundia at one extreme and pauperism, destitution and wage slavery at the other. Owing to this, disintegration and decay are quite natural there. Not so in Russia. Here agriculture cannot develop along such a path, if for no other reason than that the existence of Soviet power and the nationalisation of the principal instruments and means of production preclude such a development. In Russia the development of agriculture must proceed along a different path, along the path of organising millions of small and middle peasants in co-operatives, along the path of developing in the countryside a mass co-operative movement supported by the state by means of preferential credits. Lenin rightly pointed out in his articles on co-operation that the development of agriculture in our country must proceed along a new path, along the path of drawing the majority of the peasants into socialist construction through the co-operatives, along the path of gradually introducing into agriculture the principles of collectivism, first in the sphere of marketing and later in the sphere of production of agriculture products.

Of extreme interest in this respect are several new phenomena observed in the countryside in connection with the work of the agricultural co-operatives. It is well known that new, large organisations have sprung up within the Selskosoyuz,[18] in different branches of agriculture, such as production of flax, potatoes, butter, etc., which have a great future before them. Of these, the Flax Centre, for instance, unites a whole network of peasant flax growers' associations. The Flax Centre supplies the peasants with seeds and implements; then it buys all the flax produced by these peasants, disposes of it on the market on a large scale, guarantees the peasants a share in the profits, and in this way links peasant economy with state industry through the Selskosoyouz. What shall we call this form of organisation of production? In my opinion, it is the domestic system of large-scale state-socialist production in the sphere of agriculture. In speaking of the domestic system of state-socialist production I do so by analogy with the domestic system under capitalism, let us say, in the textile industry, where the handicraftsmen received their raw material and tools from the capitalist and turned over to him the entire product of their labour, thus being in fact semi-wage earners working in their own homes. This is one of numerous indices showing the path along which our agriculture must develop. There is no need to mention here similar indices in other branches of agriculture.

It scarcely needs proof that the vast majority of the peasantry will eagerly take this new path of development, rejecting the path of private capitalist latifundia and wage slavery, the path of destitution and ruin.

Here is what Lenin says about the path of development of our agriculture:

"State power over all large-scale means of production, state power in the hands of the proletariat, the alliance of this proletariat with the many millions of small and very small peasants, the assured leadership of the peasantry by the proletariat, etc. – is not this all that is necessary for building a complete socialist society from the co-operatives, from the co-operatives alone, which we formerly looked upon as huckstering and which from a certain aspect we have the right to look down upon as such now, under the NEP? Is this not all that is necessary for building a complete socialist society? This is not yet the building of socialist society, but it is all that is necessary and sufficient for this building" (see Vol. XXVII, p. 392).[*]

Further on, speaking of the necessity of giving financial and other assistance to the co-operatives, as a "new principle of organising the population" and a new "social system" under the dictatorship of the proletariat, Lenin continues:

"Every social system arises only with the financial assistance of a definite class. There is no need to mention the hundreds and hundreds of millions of roubles that the birth of 'free' capitalism cost. Now we must realise, and apply in our practical work, the fact that the social system which we must now give more than usual assistance is the co-operative system. But it must be assisted in the real sense of the word, i.e., it will not be enough to interpret assistance to mean assistance for any kind of co-operative trade; by assistance we must mean assistance for co-operative trade in which *really large masses of the population really take part*" (*ibid.*, p. 393).

What do all these facts prove?

That the sceptics are wrong.

That Leninism is right in regarding the masses of labouring peasants as the reserve of the proletariat.

That the proletariat in power can and must use this reserve in order to link industry with agriculture, to advance socialist construction, and to provide for the dictatorship of the proletariat that necessary foundation without which the transition to socialist economy is impossible.

---

[*] "On Co-operation," January 1923.

VI

THE NATIONAL QUESTION

From this theme I take two main questions:

a) the presentation of the question;

b) the liberation movement of the oppressed peoples and the proletarian revolution.

1) *The presentation of the question.* During the last two decades the national question has undergone a number of very important changes. The national question in the period of the Second International and the national question in the period of Leninism are far from being the same thing. They differ profoundly from each other, not only in their scope, but also in their intrinsic character.

Formerly, the national question was usually confined to a narrow circle of questions, concerning, primarily, "civilised" nationalities. The Irish, the Hungarians, the Poles, the Finns, the Serbs, and several other European nationalities – that was the circle of unequal peoples in whose destinies the leaders of the Second International were interested. The scores and hundreds of millions of Asiatic and African peoples who are suffering national oppression in its most savage and cruel form usually remained outside of their field of vision. They hesitated to put white and black, "civilised" and "uncivilised" on the same plane. Two or three meaningless, lukewarm resolutions, which carefully evaded the question of liberating the colonies – that was all the leaders of the Second International could boast of. Now we can say that this duplicity and half-heartedness in dealing with the national question has been brought to an end. Leninism laid bare this crying incongruity, broke down the wall between whites and blacks, between Europeans and Asiatics, between the "civilised" and "uncivilised" slaves of imperialism, and thus linked the national question with the question of the colonies. The national question was thereby transformed from a particular and internal state problem into a general and international problem, into a world problem of emancipating the oppressed peoples in the dependent countries and colonies from the yoke of imperialism.

Formerly, the principle of self-determination of nations was usually misinterpreted, and not infrequently it was narrowed down to the idea of the right of nations to autonomy. Certain leaders of the Second International even went so far as to turn the right to self-determination into the right to cultural autonomy, i.e., the right of oppressed nations to have their own cultural institutions, leaving all political power in the hands of the ruling nation. As a consequence, the idea of self-determination stood in danger of being transformed from an instrument for combating annexations into an instrument for justifying them. Now we can say that this confusion has been cleared up. Leninism broadened the conception of self-determinism, interpreting it as the right of the oppressed peoples of the dependent countries and colonies to complete secession, as the right of nations to independent existence as states. This precluded the possibility of justifying annexations by interpreting the right to self-determinism as the right to autonomy. Thus, the principle of self-determinism itself was transformed from an instrument for deceiving the masses, which it undoubtedly was in the hands of the social-chauvinists during the imperialist war, into an instrument for exposing all imperialist aspirations and chauvinist machinations, into an instrument for the political education of the masses in the spirit of internationalism.

Formerly, the question of the oppressed nations was usually regarded as purely a juridical question. Solemn proclamations about "national equality of rights," innumerable declarations about the "equality of nations" – that was the stock-in-trade of the parties of the Second International, which glossed over the fact that "equality of nations" under imperialism, where one group of nations (a minority) lives by exploiting another group of nations, is sheer mockery of the oppressed nations. Now we can say that this bourgeois-juridical point of view on the national question has been exposed. Leninism brought the national question down from the lofty heights of high-sounding declarations to solid ground, and declared that pronouncements about the "equality of nations" not backed by the direct support of the proletarian parties for the liberation struggle of the oppressed nations are meaningless and false. In this way the question of the oppressed nations became one of supporting the oppressed nations, of rendering real and continuous assistance to them in their struggle against imperialism for real equality of nations, for their independent existence as states.

Formerly, the national question was regarded from a reformist point of view, as an independent question having no connection with the general question of the power of capital, of the overthrow of imperialism, of the proletarian revolution. It was tacitly assumed that the victory of the proletariat in Europe was possible without a direct alliance with the liberation movement in the colonies, that the national-colonial question could be solved on the quiet, "of its own accord," off the highway of the proletarian revolution, without a revolutionary struggle against imperialism. Now we can say that this anti-revolutionary point of view has been exposed. Leninism has proved, and the imperialist war and the revolution in Russia have confirmed, that the national question can be solved only in connection with and on the basis of the proletarian revolution, and that the road to victory of the revolution in the West lies through the revolutionary alliance with the liberation movement of the colonies and dependent countries against imperialism. The national question is a part of the general question of the proletarian revolution, a part of the question of the dictatorship of the proletariat.

The question is as follows: Are the revolutionary potentialities latent in the revolutionary liberation movement of the oppressed countries *already exhausted*, or not; and if not, is there any hope, any basis, for utilising these potentialities for the proletarian revolution, for transforming the dependent and colonial countries from a reserve of the imperialist bourgeoisie into a reserve of the revolutionary proletariat, into an ally of the latter?

Leninism replies to this question in the affirmative, i.e., it recognises the existence of revolutionary capacities in the national liberation movement of the oppressed countries, and the possibility of using these for overthrowing the common enemy, for overthrowing imperialism. The mechanics of the development of imperialism, the imperialist war and the revolution in Russia wholly confirm the conclusions of Leninism on this score.

Hence the necessity for the proletariat of the "dominant" nations to support – resolutely and actively to support – the national liberation movement of the oppressed and dependent peoples.

This does not mean, of course, that the proletariat must support *every* national movement, everywhere and always, in every individual concrete case. It means that support must be given to such national movements as tend to weaken, to overthrow imperialism, and not to strengthen and preserve it. Cases occur when the national movements in certain oppressed countries came into conflict with the interests of the development of the proletarian movement. In such cases support is, of course, entirely out of the question. The question of the rights of nations is not an isolated, self-sufficient question; it is a part of the general problem of the proletarian revolution, subordinate to the whole, and must be considered from the point of view of the whole. In the forties of the last century Marx supported the national movement of the Poles and Hungarians and was opposed to the national movement of the Czechs and the South Slavs. Why? Because the Czechs and the South Slavs were then "reactionary peoples," "Russian outposts" in Europe, outposts of absolutism; whereas the Poles and the Hungarians were "revolutionary peoples," fighting against absolutism. Because support of the national movement of the Czechs and the South Slavs was at that time equivalent to indirect support for tsarism, the most dangerous enemy of the revolutionary movement in Europe.

"The various demands of democracy," writes Lenin, "including self-determination, are not an absolute, but a *small part* of the general democratic (now: general socialist) *world* movement. In individual concrete cases, the part may contradict the whole; if so, it must be rejected" (see Vol. XIX, pp. 257-58).[*]

This is the position in regard to the question of particular national movements, of the possible reactionary character of these movements – if, of course, they are appraised not from the formal point of view, not from the point of view of abstract rights, but concretely, from the point of view of the interests of the revolutionary movement.

The same must be said of the revolutionary character of national movements in general. The unquestionably revolutionary character of the vast majority of national movements is as relative and peculiar as is the possible reactionary character of certain particular national movements. The revolutionary character of a national movement under the conditions of imperialist oppression does not necessarily presuppose the existence of proletarian elements in the movement, the existence of a revolutionary or a republican programme of the movement, the existence of a democratic basis of the movement. The struggle that the Emir of Afghanistan is waging for the independence of

[*] "The Discussion on Self-Determination Summed Up," July 1916.

Afghanistan is objectively a *revolutionary* struggle, despite the monarchist views of the Emir and his associates, for it weakens, disintegrates and undermines imperialism; whereas the struggle waged by such "desperate" democrats and "socialists," "revolutionaries" and republicans as, for example, Kerensky and Tsereteli, Renaudel and Scheidemann, Chernov and Dan, Henderson and Clynes, during the imperialist war was a *reactionary* struggle, for its results was the embellishment, the strengthening, the victory, of imperialism. For the same reasons, the struggle that the Egyptians merchants and bourgeois intellectuals are waging for the independence of Egypt is objectively a *revolutionary* struggle, despite the bourgeois origin and bourgeois title of the leaders of the Egyptian national movement, despite the fact that they are opposed to socialism; whereas the struggle that the British "Labour" Government is waging to preserve Egypt's dependent position is for the same reason a *reactionary* struggle, despite the proletarian origin and the proletarian title of the members of the government, despite the fact that they are "for" socialism. There is no need to mention the national movement in other, larger, colonial and dependent countries, such as India and China, every step of which along the road to liberation, even if it runs counter to the demands of formal democracy, is a steam-hammer blow at imperialism, i.e., is undoubtedly a *revolutionary* step.

Lenin was right in saying that the national movement of the oppressed countries should be appraised not from the point of view of formal democracy, but from the point of view of the actual results, as shown by the general balance sheet of the struggle against imperialism, that is to say, "not in isolation, but on a world scale" (see Vol. XIX, p. 257).[*]

---

[*] Ibid.

2) *The liberation movement of the oppressed peoples and the proletarian revolution.* In solving the national question Leninism proceeds from the following theses:

a) The world is divided into two camps: the camp of a handful of civilised nations, which possess finance capital and exploit the vast majority of the population of the globe; and the camp of the oppressed and exploited peoples in the colonies and dependent countries, which constitute the majority.

b) The colonies and the dependent countries, oppressed and exploited by finance capital, constitute a vast reserve and a very important source of strength for imperialism.

c) The revolutionary struggle of the oppressed peoples in the dependent and colonial countries against imperialism is the only road that leads to their emancipation from oppression and exploitation.

d) The most important colonial and dependent countries have already taken the path of the national liberation movement, which cannot but lead to the crisis of world capitalism.

e) The interests of the proletarian movement in the developed countries and of the national liberation movement in the colonies call for the union of these two forms of the revolutionary movement into a common front against the common enemy, against imperialism.

f) The victory of the working class in the developed countries and the liberation of the oppressed peoples from the yoke of imperialism are impossible without the formation and the consolidation of a common revolutionary front.

g) The formation of a common revolutionary front is impossible unless the proletariat of the oppressor nations renders direct and determined support to the liberation movement of the oppressed peoples against the imperialism of its "own country," for "no nation can be free if it oppresses other nations" (*Engels*).

h) This support implies the upholding, defence and implementation of the slogan of the right of nations to secession, to independent existence as states.

i) Unless this slogan is implemented, the union and collaboration of nations within a single world economic system, which is the material basis for the victory of world socialism, cannot be brought about.

j) This union can only be voluntary, arising on the basis of mutual confidence and fraternal relations among peoples.

Hence the two sides, the two tendencies in the national question: the tendency towards political emancipation from the shackles of imperialism and towards the formation of an independent national state – a tendency which arose as a consequence of imperialist oppression and colonial exploitation; and the tendency towards closer economic relations among nations, which arose as a result of the formation of a world market and a world economic system.

"Developing capitalism," says Lenin, "knows two historical tendencies in the national question. First: the awakening of national life and national movements, struggle against all national oppression, creation of national states. Second: development and acceleration of all kinds of intercourse between nations, breakdown of national barriers, creation of the international unity of capital, of economic life in general, of politics, science, etc.

"Both tendencies are a world-wide law of capitalism. The first predominates at the beginning of its development, the second characterises mature capitalism that is moving towards its transformation into socialist society" (see Vol. XVII, pp. 139-40).[*]

For imperialism these two tendencies represent irreconcilable contradictions; because imperialism cannot exist without exploiting colonies and forcibly retaining them within the framework of the "integral whole"; because imperialism can

_____

[*] "Critical Remarks on the National Question," October-December 1913.

bring nations together only by means of annexations and colonial conquest, without which imperialism is, generally speaking, inconceivable.

For communism, on the contrary, these tendencies are but two sides of a single cause – the cause of the emancipation of the oppressed people from the yoke of imperialism; because communism knows that the union of peoples in a single world economic system is possible only in the basis of mutual confidence and voluntary agreement, and that the road to the formation of a voluntary union of peoples lies through the separation of the colonies from the "integral" imperialist "whole," through the transformation of the colonies into independent states.

Hence the necessity for a stubborn, continuous and determined struggle against the dominant-nation chauvinism of the "Socialists" of the ruling nations (Britain, France, America, Italy, Japan, etc.), who do not want to fight their imperialist governments, who do not want to support the struggle of the oppressed peoples in "their" colonies for emancipation from oppression, for secession.

Without such a struggle the education of the working class of the ruling nations in the spirit of true internationalism, in the spirit of closer relations with the toiling masses of the dependent countries and colonies, in the spirit of real preparation for the proletarian revolution, is inconceivable. The revolution would not have been victorious in Russia, and Kolchak and Denikin would not have been crushed, had not the Russian proletariat enjoyed the sympathy and support of the oppressed peoples of the former Russian Empire. But to win the sympathy and support of these peoples it had first of all to break the fetters of Russian imperialism and free these people from the yoke of national oppression.

Without this it would have been impossible to consolidate Soviet power, to implant real internationalism and to create that remarkable organisation for the collaboration of peoples which is called the Union of Soviet Socialist Republics, and which is the living prototype of the future union of peoples in a single world economic system.

Hence the necessity of fighting against the national isolationism, narrow-mindedness and aloofness of the Socialists in the oppressed countries, who do not want to rise above their national parochialism and who do not understand the connection between the liberation movement in their own countries and the proletarian movement in the ruling countries.

Without such a struggle it is inconceivable that the proletariat of the oppressed nations can maintain an independent policy and its class solidarity with the proletariat of the ruling countries in the fight for the overthrow of the common enemy, in the fight for the overthrow of imperialism.

Without such a struggle, internationalism would be impossible.

Such is the way in which the toiling masses of the dominant and of the oppressed nations must be educated in the spirit of revolutionary internationalism.

Here is what Lenin says about this twofold task of communism in educating the workers in the spirit of internationalism:

"Can such education... be *concretely identical* in great, oppressing nations and in small, oppressed nations, in annexing nations and in annexed nations?

"Obviously not. The way to the one goal – to complete equality, to the closest relations and the subsequent *amalgamation of all nations* – obviously proceeds here by different routes in each concrete case; in the same way, let us say, as the route to a point in the middle of a given page lies towards the left from one edge and towards the right from the opposite edge. If a Social-Democrat belonging to a great, oppressing, annexing nation, while advocating the amalgamation of nations in general, were to forget even for one moment that 'his' Nicholas II, 'his' Wilhelm, George, Poincare, etc., *also stands for amalgamation* with small nations (by means of annexations) – Nicholas II being for 'amalgamation' with Galicia, Wilhelm II for 'amalgamation' with Belgium, etc. – such a Social-Democrat would be a ridiculous doctrinaire in theory and an abettor of imperialism in practice.

"The weight of emphasis in the internationalist education of the workers in the oppressing countries must necessarily consist in their advocating and upholding freedom of secession for oppressed countries. Without this there can be *no* internationalism. It is our right and duty to treat every Social-Democrat of an oppressing nation who *fails* to conduct such propaganda as an imperialist and a scoundrel. This is an absolute demand, even if the *chance* of secession being possible and 'feasible' before the introduction of socialism be only one in a thousand....

"On the other hand, a Social-Democrat belonging to a small nation must emphasise in his agitation the *second* word of our general formula: 'voluntary *union*' of nations. He may, without violating his duties as an internationalist, be in favour of *either* the political independence of his nation or its inclusion in a neighbouring state X, Y, Z, etc. But in all cases he must fight *against* small-nation narrowmindedness, isolationism and aloofness, he must fight for the recognition of the whole and the general, for the subordination of the interests of the particular to the interests of the general.

"People who have not gone thoroughly into the question think there is a 'contradiction' in Social-Democrats of oppressing nations insisting on 'freedom of *secession*,' while Social-Democrats of oppressed nations insist on 'freedom of *union*.' However, a little reflection will show that there is not, and cannot be, any *other* road leading from the *given* situation to internationalism and the amalgamation of nations, any other road to this goal" (see Vol. XIX, pp. 261-62).[*]

---

[*] "The Discussion on Self-Determination Summed Up."

VII

STRATEGY AND TACTICS

From this theme I take six questions:

a) strategy and tactics as the science of leadership in the class struggle of the proletariat;

b) stages of the revolution, and strategy;

c) the flow and ebb of the movement, and tactics;

d) strategic leadership;

e) tactical leadership;

f) reformism and revolutionism.

1) *Strategy and tactics as the science of leadership in the class struggle of the proletariat.* The period of the domination of the Second International was mainly a period of the formation and training of the proletarian political armies under conditions of more or less peaceful development. It was the period of parliamentarism as the predominant form of the class struggle. Questions of great class conflicts, of preparing the proletariat for revolutionary clashes, of the means of achieving the dictatorship of the proletariat, did not seem to be on the order of the day at that time. The task was confined to utilising all means of legal development for the purpose of forming and training the proletarian armies, to utilising parliamentarism in conformity with the conditions under which the status of the proletariat remained, and, as it seemed, had to remain, that of an opposition. It scarcely needs proof that in such a period and with such a conception of the tasks of the proletariat there could be neither an integral strategy nor any elaborated tactics. There were fragmentary and detached ideas about tactics and strategy, but no tactics or strategy as such.

The mortal sin of the Second International was not that it pursued at that time the tactics of utilising parliamentary forms of struggle, but that it overestimated the importance of these forms, that it considered them virtually the only forms; and that when the period of open revolutionary battles set in and the question of extra-parliamentary forms of struggle came to the fore, the parties of the Second International turned their backs on these new tasks, refused to shoulder them.

Only in the subsequent period, the period of direct action by the proletariat, the period of proletarian revolution, when the question of overthrowing the bourgeoisie became a question of immediate practical action; when the question of the reserves of the proletariat (strategy) became one of the most burning questions; when all forms of struggle and of organisation, parliamentary and extra-parliamentary (tactics), had quite clearly manifested themselves – only in this period could an integral strategy and elaborated tactics for the struggle of the proletariat be worked out. It was precisely in this period that Lenin brought out into the light of day the brilliant ideas of Marx and Engels on tactics and strategy that been suppressed by the opportunists of the Second International. But Lenin did not confine himself to restoring particular tactical propositions of Marx and Engels. He developed them further and supplemented them with new ideas and propositions, combining them all into a system of rules and guiding principles for the leadership of the class struggle of the proletariat. Lenin's pamphlets, such as *What Is To Be Done?*, *Two Tactics*, *Imperialism*, *The State and Revolution*, *The Proletarian Revolution and the Renegade Kautsky*, *"Left Wing" Communism*, undoubtedly constitute priceless contributions to the general treasury of Marxism, to its revolutionary arsenal. The strategy and tactics of Leninism constitute the science of leadership in the revolutionary struggle of the proletariat.

2) *Stages of the revolution, and strategy.* Strategy is the determination of the direction of the main blow of the proletariat at a given stage of the revolution, the elaboration of a corresponding plan for the disposition of the revolutionary forces (main and secondary reserves), the fight to carry out this plan throughout the given stage of the revolution.

Our revolution had already passed through two stages, and after the October Revolution it entered a third one. Our strategy changed accordingly.

First stage. 1903 to February 1917. Objective: to overthrow tsarism and completely wipe out the survivals of mediaevalism. The main force of the revolution: the proletariat. Immediate reserves: the peasantry. Direction of the main blow: the isolation of the liberal-monarchist bourgeoisie, which was striving to win over the peasantry and liquidate the revolution by a *compromise* with tsarism. Plan for the disposition of forces: alliance of the working class with the peasantry. "The proletariat must carry to completion the democratic revolution, by allying to itself the mass of the peasantry in order to crush by force the resistance of the autocracy and to paralyse the instability of the bourgeoisie" (see Lenin, Vol. VIII, p. 96).[*]

Second stage. March 1917 to October 1917. Objective: to overthrow imperialism in Russia and to withdraw from the imperialist war. The main force of the revolution: the proletariat. Immediate reserves: the poor peasantry. The proletariat of neighbouring countries as probable reserves. The protracted war and the crisis of imperialism as a favourable factor. Direction of the main blow: isolation of the petty-bourgeois democrats (Mensheviks and Socialist-Revolutionaries), who were striving to win over the toiling masses of the peasantry and to put an end to the revolution by a *compromise* with imperialism. Plan

---

[*] "Two Tactics of Social-Democracy in the Democratic Revolution," June-July 1905.

for the disposition of forces: alliance of the proletariat with the poor peasantry. "The proletariat must accomplish the socialist revolution, by allying to itself the mass of the semi-proletarian elements of the population in order to crush by force the resistance of the bourgeoisie and to paralyse the instability of the peasantry and the petty bourgeoisie" (*ibid.*).

Third stage. Began after the October Revolution. Objective: to consolidate the dictatorship of the proletariat in one country, using it as a base for the defeat of imperialism in all countries. The revolution spreads beyond the confines of one country; the epoch of world revolution has begun. The main force of the revolution: the dictatorship of the proletariat in one country, the revolutionary movement of the proletariat in all countries. Main reserves: the semi-proletarian and small-peasant masses in the developed countries, the liberation movement of the colonies and dependent countries. Direction of the main blow: isolation of the petty-bourgeois democrats, isolation of the parties of the Second International, which constitute the main support of the policy of *compromise* with imperialism. Plan for the disposition of forces: alliance of the proletarian revolution with the liberation movement in the colonies and the dependent countries.

Strategy deals with the main forces of the revolution and their reserves. It changes with the passing of the revolution from one stage to another, but remains basically unchanged throughout a given stage.

3) *The flow and ebb of the movement, and tactics.* Tactics are the determination of the line of conduct of the proletariat in the comparatively short period of the flow or ebb of the movement, of the rise or decline of the revolution, the fight to carry out this line by means of replacing old forms of struggle and organisation by new ones, old slogans by new ones, by combining these forms, etc. While the object of strategy is to win the war against tsarism, let us say, or against the bourgeoisie, to

carry through the struggle against tsarism or against the bourgeoisie to its end, tactics pursue less important objects, for their
aim is not the winning of the war as a whole, but the winning of
some particular engagements or some particular battles, the
carrying through successfully of some particular campaigns or
actions corresponding to the concrete circumstances in the
given period of rise or decline of the revolution. Tactics are a
part of strategy, subordinate to it and serving it.

Tactics change according to flow and ebb. While the strategic plan remained unchanged during the first stage of the revolution (1903 to February 1917), tactics changed several times
during that period. In the period from 1903 to 1905 the Party
pursued offensive tactics, for the tide of the revolution was rising, the movement was on the upgrade, and tactics had to proceed from this fact. Accordingly, the forms of struggle were
revolutionary, corresponding to the requirements of the rising
tide of the revolution. Local political strikes, political demonstrations, the general political strike, boycott of the Duma, uprising, revolutionary fighting slogans – such were the
successive forms of the struggle during that period. These
changes in the forms of struggle were accomplished by corresponding changes in the forms of organisation. Factory committees, revolutionary peasant committees, strike committees,
Soviets of workers' deputies, a workers' party operating more
or less openly – such were the forms of organisation during that
period.

In the period from 1907 to 1912 the Party was compelled to
resort to tactics of retreat; for we then experienced a decline in
the revolutionary movement, the ebb of the revolution, and tactics necessarily had to take this fact into consideration. The
forms of struggle, as well as the forms of organisation, changed
accordingly: instead of the boycott of the Duma – participation
in the Duma; instead of open revolutionary actions outside the
Duma – actions and work in the Duma; instead of general po-

litical strikes – partial economic strikes, or simply a lull in activities. Of course, the Party had to go underground during that period, while the revolutionary mass organisations were replaced by cultural, educational, co-operative, insurance and other legal organisations.

The same must be said of the second and third stages of the revolution, during which tactics changed dozens of times, whereas the strategic plans remained unchanged.

Tactics deal with the forms of struggle and the forms of organisation of the proletariat, with their changes and combinations. During a given stage of the revolution tactics may change several times, depending on the flow or ebb, the rise or decline of the revolution.

4) *Strategic leadership*. The reserves of the revolution can be:

direct: a) the peasantry and in general the intermediate strata of the population within the country; b) the proletariat of neighbouring countries; c) the revolutionary movement in the colonies and dependent countries; d) the conquests and gains of the dictatorship of the proletariat – part of which the proletariat may give up temporarily, while retaining superiority of forces, in order to buy off a powerful enemy and gain a respite; and

indirect: a) the contradictions and conflicts among the non-proletarian classes within the country, which can be utilised by the proletariat to weaken the enemy and to strengthen its own reserves; b) contradictions, conflicts and wars (the imperialist war, for instance) among the bourgeois states hostile to the proletarian state, which can be utilised by the proletariat in its offensive or in manoeuvring in the event of a forced retreat.

There is no need to speak at length about the reserves of the first category, as their significance is clear to everyone. As for the reserves of the second category, whose significance is not clear, it must be said that sometimes they are of prime importance for the progress of the revolution. One can hardly deny the enormous importance, for example, of the conflicts between the petty-bourgeois democrats (the Socialist-Revolutionaries) and the liberal-monarchists bourgeoisie (the Cadets) during and after the first revolution, which undoubtedly played its part in freeing the peasantry from the influence of the bourgeoisie. Still less reason is there for denying the colossal importance of the fact that the principal groups of imperialists were engaged in a deadly war during the period of the October Revolution, when the imperialists, engrossed in war among themselves, were unable to concentrate their forces against the young Soviet power, and the proletariat for this very reason, was able to get down to work of organising its forces and consolidating its power, and to prepare the rout of Kolchak and Denikin. It must be presumed that now, when the contradictions among the imperialist groups are becoming more and more profound, and when a new war among them is becoming inevitable, reserves of this description will assume ever greater importance for the proletariat.

The task of strategic leadership is to make proper use of all these reserves for the achievement of the main object of the revolution at the given stage of its development.

What does making proper use of reserves mean?

It means fulfilling certain necessary conditions, of which the following must be regarded as the principal ones:

Firstly. The concentration of the main forces of the revolution at the enemy's most vulnerable spot at the decisive moment, when the revolution has already become ripe, when the offensive is going full-steam ahead, when insurrection is knocking at the door, and when bringing the reserves up to the vanguard is the decisive condition of success. The Party's strategy during the period from April to October 1917 can be taken as an example of this manner of utilising reserves. Undoubtedly, the enemy's most vulnerable spot at that time was the war. Undoubtedly, it was on this question, as the fundamental one, that the Party rallied the broadest masses of the population around the proletarian vanguard. The Party's strategy during that period was, while training the vanguard for street action by means of manifestations and demonstrations, to bring the reserves up to the vanguard through the medium of the Soviets in the rear and the soldiers' committees at the front. The outcome of the revolution has shown that the reserves were properly utilised.

Here is what Lenin, paraphrasing the well-known theses of Marx and Engels on insurrection, says about this condition of the strategic utilisation of the forces of the revolution:

"1) Never *play* with insurrection, but when beginning it firmly realise that you must *go to the end*.

"2) Concentrate a *great superiority of forces* at the decisive point, at the decisive moment, otherwise the enemy, who has the advantage of better preparation and organisation, will destroy the insurgents.

"3) Once the insurrection has begun, you must act with the greatest *determination*, and by all means, without fail, take the *offensive*. 'The defensive is the death of every armed uprising.'

"4) You must try to take the enemy by surprise and seize the moment when his forces are scattered.

"5) You must strive for *daily* success, even if small (one might say hourly, if it is the case of one town), and at all costs retain the '*moral ascendancy*' " (see Vol. XXI, pp. 319-20).[*]

Secondly. The selection of the moment for the decisive blow, of the moment for starting the insurrection, so timed as to coincide with the moment when the crisis has reached its climax, when it is already the case that the vanguard is prepared to fight to the end, the reserves are prepared to support the vanguard, and maximum consternation reigns in the ranks of the enemy.

The decisive battle, says Lenin, may be deemed to have fully matured *if* "(1) all the class forces hostile to us have become sufficiently entangled, are sufficiently at loggerheads, have sufficiently weakened themselves in a struggle which is beyond their strength"; *if* "(2) all the

---

[*] "Advice of an Onlooker," October 1917.

vacillating, wavering, unstable, intermediate elements – the petty bourgeoisie, the petty-bourgeois democrats as distinct from the bourgeoisie – have sufficiently exposed themselves in the eyes of the people, have sufficiently disgraced themselves through their practical bankruptcy"; *if* "(3) among the proletariat a mass sentiment in favour of supporting the most determined, supremely bold, revolutionary action against the bourgeoisie has arisen and begun vigorously to grow. Then revolution is indeed ripe; then, indeed, if we have correctly gauged all the conditions indicated above... and if we have chosen the moment rightly, our victory is assured" (see Vol. XXV, p. 229).[*]

The manner in which the October uprising was carried out may be taken as a model of such strategy.

Failure to observe this condition leads to a dangerous error called "loss of tempo," when the Party lags behind the movement or runs far ahead of it, courting the danger of failure. An example of such "loss of tempo," of how the moment for an uprising should not be chosen, may be seen in the attempt made by a section of our comrades to begin the uprising by arresting the Democratic Conference in September 1917, when wavering was still apparent in the Soviets, when the armies at the front were still at the crossroads, when the reserves had not yet been brought up to the vanguard.

Thirdly. Undeviating pursuit of the course adopted, no matter what difficulties and complications are encountered on the road towards the goal; this is necessary in order that the vanguard may not lose sight of the main goal of the struggle and that the masses may not stray from the road while marching towards that goal and striving to rally around the vanguard. Failure to observe this condition leads to a grave error, well known to sailors as "losing one's bearing." As an example of this "losing one's bearings" we may take the erroneous conduct of our Party when, immediately after the Democratic Confer-

---

[*] " 'Left-Wing' Communism, an Infantile Disorder."

ence, it adopted a resolution to participate in the Pre-parliament. For the moment the Party, as it were, forgot that the Pre-parliament was an attempt of the bourgeoisie to switch the country from the path of the Soviets to the path of bourgeois parliamentarism, that the Party's participation in such a body might result in mixing everything up and confusing the workers and peasants, who were waging a revolutionary struggle under the slogan: "All power to the Soviets." This mistake was rectified by the withdrawal of the Bolsheviks from the Pre-parliament.

Fourthly. Manoeuvring the reserves with a view to effecting a proper retreat when the enemy is strong, when retreat is inevitable, when to accept battle forced upon us by the enemy is obviously disadvantageous, when, with the given relation of forces, retreat becomes the only way to escape a blow against the vanguard and to retain the reserves for the latter.

"The revolutionary parties," says Lenin, "must complete their education. They have learned to attack. Now they have to realise that this knowledge must be supplemented with the knowledge how to retreat properly. They have to realise – and the revolutionary class is taught to realise it by its own bitter experience – that victory is impossible unless they have learned both how to attack and how to retreat properly" (see Vol. XXV, p. 177).[*]

The object of this strategy is to gain time, to disrupt the enemy, and to accumulate forces in order to later assume the offensive.

The signing of the Brest Peace may be taken as a model of this strategy, for it enabled the Party to gain time, to take advantage of the conflicts in the camp of the imperialists, to disrupt the forces of the enemy, to retain the support of the peasantry, and to accumulate forces in preparation for the offensive against Kolchak and Denikin.

---

[*] Ibid.

"In concluding a separate peace," said Lenin at that time, "we free ourselves as much *as it is possible at the present moment* from both warring imperialist groups, we take advantage of their mutual enmity and warfare, which hinder them from making a deal against us, and for a certain period have our hands free to advance and to consolidate the socialist revolution" (see Vol. XXII, p. 198).[*]

"Now even the biggest fool," said Lenin three years after the Brest Peace, can see "that the 'Brest Peace' was a concession that strengthened us and broke up the forces of international imperialism" (see Vol. XXVII, p. 7).[†]

Such are the principal conditions which ensure correct strategic leadership.

5) *Tactical leadership.* Tactical leadership is a part of strategic leadership, subordinated to the tasks and the requirements of the latter. The task of tactical leadership is to master all forms of struggle and organisation of the proletariat and to ensure that they are used properly so as to achieve, with the given relations of forces, the maximum results necessary to prepare for strategic success.

What is meant by making proper use of the forms of struggle and organisation of the proletariat?

It means fulfilling certain necessary conditions, of which the following must be regarded as the principal ones:

Firstly. To put in the forefront precisely those forms of struggle and organisation which are best suited to the conditions prevailing during the flow or ebb of the movement at a given moment, and which therefore can facilitate and ensure the bringing of the masses to the revolutionary positions, the bringing of the millions to the revolutionary front, and their disposition at the revolutionary front.

---

[*] "On the History of the Question of the Unfortunate Peace," February 1918.
[†] "New Times and Old Mistakes in a New Guise," August 1921.

The point here is not that the vanguard should realise the impossibility of preserving the old regime and the inevitability of its overthrow. The point is that the masses, the millions, should understand this inevitability and display their readiness to support the vanguard. But the masses can understand this only from their own experience. The task is to enable the vast masses to realise from their own experience the inevitability of the overthrow of the old regime, to promote such methods of struggle and forms of organisations as will make it easier for the masses to realise from experience the correctness of the revolutionary slogans.

The vanguard would have become detached from the working class, and the working class would have lost contact with the masses, if the Party had not decided at the time to participate in the Duma, if it had not decided to concentrate its forces on work in the Duma and to develop a struggle on the basis of this work, in order to make it easier for the masses to realise from their own experience the futility of the Duma, the falsity of the promises of the Cadets, the impossibility of compromise with tsarism, and the inevitability of an alliance between the peasantry and the working class. Had the masses not gained their experience during the period of the Duma, the exposure of the Cadets and the hegemony of the proletariat would have been impossible.

The danger of the "Otzovist" [from "otziv," recall – *Red Star Publishers*] tactics was that they threatened to detach the vanguard from the millions of its reserves.

The Party would have become detached from the working class, and the working class would have lost its influence among the broad masses of the peasants and soldiers, if the proletariat had followed the "Left" Communists, who called for an uprising in April 1917, when the Mensheviks and Socialist-Revolutionaries had not yet exposed themselves as advocates of war and imperialism, when the masses had not yet realized from their own experience the falsity of speeches of the Mensheviks and Socialist-Revolutionaries about peace, land and freedom. Had the masses not gained this experience during the Kerensky period, the Mensheviks and Socialist-Revolutionaries would not have been isolated and the dictatorship of the proletariat would have been impossible. Therefore, the tactics of "patiently explaining" the mistakes of the petty-bourgeois parties and of open struggle in the Soviets were the only correct tactics.

The danger of the tactics of the "Left" Communists was that they threatened to transform the Party from the leader of the proletarian revolution into a handful of futile conspirators with no ground to stand on.

"Victory cannot be won with the vanguard alone," says Lenin. "To throw the vanguard alone into the decisive battle, before the whole class, before the broad masses have taken up a position either of direct support of the vanguard, or at least of benevolent neutrality towards it... would be not merely folly but a crime. And in order that actually the whole class, that actually the broad masses of the working people and those oppressed by capital may take up such a position, propaganda and agitation alone are not enough. For this the masses must have their own political experience. Such is the fundamental law of all great revolutions, now confirmed with astonishing force and vividness not only in Russia but also in Germany. Not only the uncultured, often illiterate masses of Russia, but the highly cultured, entirely literate masses of Germany had to realise through their own painful experience the absolute impotence and spinelessness, the absolute helplessness and servility to the bourgeoisie, the utter vileness, of the government of the knights of the Second International, the absolute inevitability of a dictatorship of the extreme reactionaries (Kornilov in Russia, Kapp[19] and Co. in Germany) as the only alternative to a dictatorship of the proletariat, in order to turn resolutely towards communism" (see Vol. XXV, p. 228).[*]

---

[*] " 'Left-Wing' Communism, an Infantile Disorder."

Secondly. To locate at any given moment the particular link in the chain of processes which, if grasped, will enable us to keep hold of the whole chain and to prepare the conditions for achieving strategic success.

The point here is to single out from all the tasks confronting the Party the particular immediate task, the fulfilment of which constitutes the central point, and the accomplishment of which ensures the successful fulfilment of the other immediate tasks.

The importance of this thesis may be illustrated by two examples, one of which could be taken from the remote past (the period of the formation of the Party) and the other from the immediate present (the period of the NEP).

In the period of the formation of the Party, when the innumerable circles and organizations had not yet been linked together, when amateurishness and the parochial outlook of the circles were corroding the Party from top to bottom, when ideological confusion was the characteristic feature of the internal life of the Party, the main link and the main task in the chain of links and in the chain of tasks then confronting the Party proved to be the establishment of an all-Russian illegal newspaper (*Iskra*). Why? Because, under the conditions then prevailing, only by means of an all-Russian illegal newspaper was it possible to create a solid core of the Party capable of uniting the innumerable circles and organisations into one whole, to prepare the conditions for ideological and tactical unity, and thus to build the foundations for the formation of a real party.

During the period of transition from war to economic construction, when industry was vegetating in the grip of disruption and agriculture was suffering from a shortage of urban manufactured goods, when the establishment of a bond between state industry and peasant economy became the fundamental condition for successful socialist construction – in that period it turned out that the main link in the chain of processes, the main task among a number of tasks, was to develop trade. Why? Because under the conditions of the NEP the bond between industry and peasant economy cannot be established except through trade; because under the conditions of the NEP production without sale is fatal for industry; because industry can be expanded only by the expansion of sales as a result of developing trade; because only after we have consolidated our position in the sphere of trade, only after we have secured control of trade, only after we have secured this link can be there be any hope of linking industry with the peasant market and successfully fulfilling the other immediate tasks in order to create the conditions for building the foundations of socialist economy.

"It is not enough to be a revolutionary and an adherent of socialism or a Communist in general," says Lenin. "One must be able at each particular moment to find the particular link in the chain which one must grasp with all one's might in order to keep hold of the whole chain and to prepare firmly for the transition to the next link...."

"At the present time... this link is the revival of internal *trade* under proper state regulation (direction). Trade – that is the 'link' in the historical chain of events, in the transitional forms of our socialist construction in 1921-22, '*which we must grasp with all our might*'..." (see Vol. XXVII, p. 82).[*]

Such are the principal conditions which ensure correct tactical leadership.

6) *Reformism and revolutionism*. What is the difference between revolutionary tactics and reformist tactics?

Some think that Leninism is opposed to reforms, opposed to compromises and to agreements in general. This is absolutely wrong. Bolsheviks know as well as anybody else that in a certain sense "every little bit helps," that under certain conditions

---

[*] "The Importance of Gold Now and After the Complete Victory of Socialism," November 1921.

reforms in general, and compromises and agreements in particular, are necessary and useful.

"To carry on a war for the overthrow of the international bourgeoisie," says Lenin, "a war which is a hundred times more difficult, protracted, and complicated than the most stubborn of ordinary wars between states, and to refuse beforehand to manoeuvre, to utilise the conflict of interests (even though temporary) among one's enemies, to reject agreements and compromises with possible (even though temporary, unstable, vacillating and conditional) allies – is not this ridiculous in the extreme? Is it not as though, when making a difficult ascent of an unexplored and hitherto inaccessible mountain, we were to refuse beforehand ever to move in zigzags, ever to retrace our steps, ever to abandon the course once selected and to try others?" (see Vol. XXV, p. 210).*

Obviously, therefore, it is not a matter of reforms or of compromises and agreements, but of the use people make of reforms and agreements.

To a reformist, reforms are everything, while revolutionary work is something incidental, something just to talk about, mere eyewash. That is why, with reformist tactics under the conditions of bourgeois rule, reforms are inevitability transformed into an instrument for strengthening that rule, an instrument for disintegrating the revolution.

To a revolutionary, on the contrary, the main thing is revolutionary work and not reforms; to him reforms are a by-product of the revolution. That is why, with revolutionary tactics under the conditions of bourgeois rule, reforms are naturally transformed into an instrument for strengthening the revolution, into a strongpoint for the further development of the revolutionary movement.

The revolutionary will accept a reform in order to use it as an aid in combining legal work with illegal work and to inten-

---

* " 'Left-Wing' Communism, an Infantile Disorder."

sify, under its cover, the illegal work for the revolutionary preparation of the masses for the overthrow of the bourgeoisie.

That is the essence of making revolutionary use of reforms and agreements under the conditions of imperialism.

The reformist, on the contrary, will accept reforms in order to renounce all illegal work, to thwart the preparation of the masses for the revolution and to rest in the shade of "bestowed" reforms.

That is the essence of reformist tactics.

Such is the position in regard to reforms and agreements under the conditions of imperialism.

The situation changes somewhat, however, after the overthrow of imperialism, under the dictatorship of the proletariat. Under certain conditions, in a certain situation, the proletarian power may find itself compelled temporarily to leave the path of the revolutionary reconstruction of the existing order of things and to take the path of its gradual transformation, the "reformist path," as Lenin says in his well-known article "The Importance of Gold,"[20] the path of flanking movements, of reforms and concessions to the non-proletarian classes – in order to disintegrate these classes, to give the revolution a respite, to recuperate one's forces and prepare the conditions for a new offensive. It cannot be denied that in a sense this is a "reformist" path. But it must be borne in mind that there is a fundamental distinction here, which consists in the fact that in this case the reform emanates from the proletarian power, it strengthens the proletarian power, it procures for it a necessary respite, its purpose is to disintegrate, not the revolution, but the non-proletarian classes.

Under such conditions a reform is thus transformed into its opposite.

The proletarian power is able to adopt such a policy because, and only because, the sweep of the revolution in the preceding period was great enough and therefore provided a sufficiently wide expanse within which to retreat, substituting for offensive tactics the tactics of temporary retreat, the tactics of flanking movements.

Thus, while formerly, under bourgeois rule, reforms were a by-product of revolution, now under the dictatorship of the proletariat, the source of reforms is the revolutionary gains of the proletariat, the reserves accumulated in the hands of the proletariat consisting of these gains.

"Only Marxism," says Lenin, "has precisely and correctly defined the relation of reforms to revolution. However, Marx was able to see this relation only from one aspect, namely, under the conditions preceding the first to any extent permanent and lasting victory of the proletariat, if only in a single country. Under those conditions, the basis of the proper relations was: reforms are a by-product of the revolutionary class struggle of the proletariat... After the victory of the proletariat, if only in a single country, something new enters into the relation between reforms and revolution. In principle, it is the same as before, but a change in form takes place, which Marx himself could not foresee, but which can be appreciated only on the basis of the philosophy and politics of Marxism... After the victory (while still remaining a 'by-product' on an international scale) they (i.e., reforms – *J. St.*) are, in addition, for the country in which victory has been achieved, a necessary and legitimate respite in those cases when, after the utmost exertion of effort, it becomes obvious that sufficient strength is lacking for the revolutionary accomplishment of this or that transition. Victory creates such a 'reserve of strength' that it is possible to hold out even in a forced retreat, to hold out both materially and morally" (see Vol. XXVII, pp. 84-85).[*]

---

[*] "The Importance of Gold Now and After the Complete Victory of Socialism."

VIII

THE PARTY

In the pre-revolutionary period, the period of more or less peaceful development, when the parties of the Second International were the predominant force in the working-class movement and parliamentary forms of struggle were regarded as the principal forms – under these conditions the Party neither had nor could have had that great and decisive importance which it acquired afterwards, under conditions of open revolutionary clashes. Defending the Second International against attacks made upon it, Kautsky says that the parties of the Second International are an instrument of peace and not of war, and that for this very reason they were powerless to take any important steps during the war, during the period of revolutionary action by the proletariat. That is quite true. But what does it mean? It means that the parties of the Second International are unfit for the revolutionary struggle of the proletariat, that they are not militant parties of the proletariat, leading the workers to power, but election machines adapted for parliamentary elections and parliamentary struggle. This, in fact, explains why, in the days when the opportunists of the Second International were in the ascendancy, it was not the party but its parliamentary group that was the chief political organisation of the proletariat. It is well known that the party at that time was really an appendage and subsidiary of the parliamentary group. It scarcely needs proof that under such circumstances and with such a party at the helm there could be no question of preparing the proletariat for revolution.

But matters have changed radically with the dawn of the new period. The new period is one of open class collisions, of revolutionary action by the proletariat, of proletarian revolution, a period when forces are being directly mustered for the overthrow of imperialism and the seizure of power by the proletariat. In this period the proletariat is confronted with new tasks, the tasks of reorganising all party work on new, revolutionary lines; of educating the workers in the spirit of revolutionary struggle for power; of preparing and moving up reserves; of establishing an alliance with the proletarians of neighbouring countries; of establishing firm ties with the liberation movement in the colonies and dependent countries, etc., etc. To think that these new tasks can be performed by the old Social-Democratic parties, brought up as they were in the peaceful conditions of parliamentarism, is to doom oneself to hopeless despair, to inevitable defeat. If, with such tasks to shoulder, the proletariat remained under the leadership of the old parties, it would be completely unarmed. It scarcely needs proof that the proletariat could not consent to such a state of affairs.

Hence the necessity for a new party, a militant party, a revolutionary party, one bold enough to lead the proletarians in the struggle for power, sufficiently experienced to find its bearings amidst the complex conditions of a revolutionary situation, and sufficiently flexible to steer clear of all submerged rocks in the path to its goal.

Without such a party it is useless even to think of overthrowing imperialism, of achieving the dictatorship of the proletariat.

This new party is the party of Leninism.

What are the specific features of this new party?

1) *The Party as the advanced detachment of the working class.* The Party must be, first of all, the *advanced* detachment of the working class. The Party must absorb all the best elements of the working class, their experience, their revolutionary spirit, their selfless devotion to the cause of the proletariat. But in order that it may really be the armed detachment, the Party must be armed with revolutionary theory, with a knowledge of

the laws of the movement, with a knowledge of the laws of revolution. Without this it will be incapable of directing the struggle of the proletariat, of leading the proletariat. The Party cannot be a real party if it limits itself to registering what the masses of the working class feel and think, if it drags at the tail of the spontaneous movement, if it is unable to overcome the inertia and the political indifference of the spontaneous movement, if it is unable to rise above the momentary interests of the proletariat, if it is unable to raise the masses to the level of understanding the class interests of the proletariat. The Party must stand at the head of the working class; it must see farther than the working class; it must lead the proletariat, and not drag at the tail of the spontaneous movement. The parties of the Second International, which preach "khvostism," are vehicles of bourgeois policy, which condemns the proletariat to the role of a tool in the hands of the bourgeoisie. Only a party which adopts the standpoint of advanced detachment of the proletariat and is able to raise the masses to the level of understanding the class interest of the proletariat – only such a party can divert the working class from the path of trade unionism and convert it into an independent political force.

The Party is the political leader of the working class.

I have already spoken of the difficulties of the struggle of the working class, of the complicated conditions of the struggle, of strategy and tactics, of reserves and manoeuvring, of attack and retreat. These conditions are no less complicated, if not more so, than the conditions of war. Who can see clearly in these conditions, who can give correct guidance to the proletarian millions? No army at war can dispense with an experienced General Staff if it does not want to be doomed to defeat. Is it not clear that the proletariat can still less dispense with such a General Staff if it does not want to allow itself to be devoured by its mortal enemies? But where is this General Staff? Only the revolutionary party of the proletariat can serve as this General Staff. The working class without a revolutionary party is an army without a General Staff.

The Party is the General Staff of the proletariat.

But the Party cannot be only an *advanced* detachment. It must at the same time be a detachment of the *class*, part of the class, closely bound up with it by all the fibres of its being. The distinction between the advanced detachment and the rest of the working class, between Party members and non-Party people, cannot disappear until classes disappear; it will exist as long as the ranks of the proletariat continue to be replenished with former members of other classes, as long as the working class as a whole is not in a position to rise to the level of the advanced detachment. But the Party would cease to be a party if this distinction developed into a gap, if the Party turned in on itself and became divorced from the non-Party masses. The Party cannot lead the class if it is not connected with the non-Party masses, if there is no bond between the Party and the non-Party masses, if these masses do not accept its leadership, if the Party enjoys no moral and political credit among the masses.

Recently 200,000 new members from the ranks of the workers were admitted into our Party. The remarkable thing about this is the fact that these people did not merely join the Party themselves, but were rather sent there by all the rest of the non-Party workers, who took an active part in the admission of the new members, and without whose approval no new member was accepted. This fact shows that the broad masses of non-Party workers regard our Party as *their* Party, as a Party *near* and *dear* to them, in whose expansion and consolidation they are vitally interested and to whose leadership they voluntarily entrust their destiny. It scarcely needs proof that without these intangible moral threads which connect the Party with the non-Party masses, the Party could not have become the decisive force of its class.

The Party is an inseparable part of the working class.

"We," says Lenin, "are the Party of a class, and therefore *almost the whole class* (and in times of war, in the period of civil war, the whole class) should act under the leadership of our Party, should adhere to our Party as closely as possible. But it would be Manilovism[21] and 'khvostism' to think that at any time under capitalism almost the whole class, or the whole class, would be able to rise to the level of consciousness and activity of its advanced detachment, of its Social-Democratic Party. No sensible Social-Democrat has ever yet doubted that under capitalism even the trade union organisations (which are more primitive and more comprehensible to the undeveloped strata) are unable to embrace almost the whole, or the whole, working class. To forget the distinction between the advanced detachment and the whole of the masses which gravitate towards it, to forget the constant duty of the advanced detachment to *raise* ever wider strata to this most advanced level, means merely to deceive oneself, to shut one's eyes to the immensity of our tasks, and to narrow down these tasks" (see Vol. VI, pp. 205-06).[*]

2) *The Party as the organised detachment of the working class.* The Party is not only the *advanced* detachment of the working class. If it desires really to direct the struggle of the class it must at the same time be the *organised* detachment of its class. The Party's tasks under the conditions of capitalism are immense and extremely varied. The Party must direct the struggle of the proletariat under the exceptionally difficult conditions of internal and external development; it must lead the proletariat in the offensive when the situation calls for an offensive; it must lead the proletariat so as to escape the blow of a powerful enemy when the situation calls for retreat; it must imbue the millions of unorganised non-Party workers with the spirit of organisation and endurance. But the Party can fulfil these tasks only if it is itself the embodiment of discipline and organisation, if it is itself the *organised* detachment of the proletariat. Without these conditions there can be no question of the Party really leading the vast masses of the proletariat.

---

[*] "One Step Forward, Two Steps Back," February-May 1904.

The Party is the organised detachment of the working class.

The conception of the Party as an organised whole is embodied in Lenin's well-known formulation of the first paragraph of our Party Rules, in which the Party is regarded as the *sum total* of its organisations, and the Party member as a member of one of the organisations of the Party. The Mensheviks, who objected to this formulation as early as 1903, proposed to substitute for it a "system" of self-enrolment in the Party, a "system" of conferring the "title" of Party member upon every "professor" and "high-school student," upon every "sympathiser" and "striker" who supported the Party in one way or another, but who did not join and did not want to join any one of the Party organisations. It scarcely needs proof that had this singular "system" become entrenched in our Party it would inevitably have led to our Party becoming inundated with professors and high-school students and to its degeneration into a loose, amorphous, disorganised "formation," lost in a sea of "sympathisers," that would have obliterated the dividing line between the Party and the class and would have upset the Party's task of raising the unorganised masses to the level of the advanced detachment. Needless to say, under such an opportunist "system" our Party would have been unable to fulfil the role of the organising core of the working class in the course of our revolution.

"From the point of view of Comrade Martov," says Lenin, "the border-line of the Party remains quite indefinite, for 'every striker' may 'proclaim himself a Party member.' What is the use of this vagueness? A wide extension of the 'title.' Its harm is that it introduces a *disorganising* idea, the confusing of class and Party" (see Vol. VI, p. 211).*

But the Party is not merely the *sum total* of Party organisations. The Party is at the same time a single *system* of these or-

---

* Ibid.

ganisations, their formal union into a single whole, with higher and lower leading bodies, with subordination of the minority to the majority, with practical decisions binding on all members of the Party. Without these conditions the Party cannot be a single organised whole capable of exercising systematic and organised leadership in the struggle of the working class.

"*Formerly*," says Lenin, "our Party was not a formally organized whole, but only the sum of separate groups, and therefore no other relations except those of ideological influence were possible between these groups. *Now* we have become an organized Party, and this implies the establishment of authority, the transformation of the power of ideas into the power of authority, the subordination of lower Party bodies to higher Party bodies" (see Vol. VI, p. 291).[*]

The principle of the minority submitting to the majority, the principle of directing Party work from a centre, not infrequently gives rise to attacks on the part of wavering elements, to accusations of "bureaucracy," "formalism," etc. It scarcely needs proof that systematic work by the Party as one whole, and the directing of the struggle of the working class, would be impossible without putting these principles into effect. Leninism in questions of organisation is the unswerving application of these principles. Lenin terms the fight against these principles "Russian nihilism" and "aristocratic anarchism," which deserves to be ridiculed and swept aside.

Here is what Lenin says about these wavering elements in his book *One Step Forward*:

"This aristocratic anarchism is particularly characteristic of the Russian nihilist. He thinks of the Party organisation as a monstrous 'factory'; he regards the subordination of the part to the whole and of the minority to the majority as 'serfdom'..., division of labour under the direction of a centre evokes from him a tragi-comical outcry against people being transformed into 'wheels and cogs'..., mention of

---

[*] Ibid.

the organisational rules of the Party calls forth a contemptuous grimace and the disdainful... remark that one could very well dispense with rules altogether."

"It is clear, I think, that the cries about this celebrated bureaucracy are just a screen for dissatisfaction with the personal composition of the central bodies, a fig leaf.... You are a bureaucrat because you were appointed by the congress not by my will, but against it; you are a formalist because you rely on the formal decisions of the congress, and not on my consent; you are acting in a grossly mechanical way because you plead the 'mechanical' majority at the Party Congress and pay no heed to my wish to be co-opted; you are an autocrat because you refuse to hand over the power to the old gang." [The "gang" here referred to is that of Axelrod, Martov, Potresov and others, who would not submit to the decisions of the Second Congress and who accused Lenin of being a "bureaucrat." – *J. St.*] (See Vol. VI, pp. 310, 287.)

3) *The Party as the highest form of class organisation of the proletariat.* The Party is the organised detachment of the working class. But the Party is not the only organisation of the working class. The proletariat has also a number of other organisations, without which it cannot wage a successful struggle against capital: trade unions, co-operatives, factory organisations, parliamentary groups, non-Party women's associations, the press, cultural and educational organisations, youth leagues, revolutionary fighting organisations (in times of open revolutionary action), Soviets of deputies as the form of state organisation (if the proletariat is in power), etc. The overwhelming majority of these organisations are non-Party, and only some of them adhere directly to the Party, or constitute offshoots from it. All these organisations, under certain conditions, are absolutely necessary for the working class, for without them it would be impossible to consolidate the class positions of the proletariat in the diverse spheres of struggle; for without them it would be impossible to steel the proletariat as the force whose mission it is to replace the bourgeois order by the socialist order. But how can single leadership be exercised with such an

abundance or organisations? What guarantee is there that this multiplicity of organisations will not lead to divergency in leadership? It may be said that each of these organisations carries on its work in its own special field, and that therefore these organisations cannot hinder one another. That, of course, is true. But it is also true that all these organisations should work in one direction for they serve *one* class, the class of the proletarians. The question then arises: who is to determine the line, the general direction, along which the work of all these organisations is to be conducted? Where is the central organisations which is not only able, because it has the necessary experience, to work out such a general line, but, in addition, is in a position, because it has sufficient prestige, to induce all these organisations to carry out this line, so as to attain unity of leadership and to make hitches impossible?

That organisation is the Party of the proletariat.

The Party possesses all the necessary qualifications for this because, in the first place, it is the rallying centre of the finest elements in the working class, who have direct connections with the non-Party organisations of the proletariat and very frequently lead them; because, secondly, the Party, as the rallying centre of the finest members of the working class, is the best school for training leaders of the working class, capable of directing every form of organisation of their class; because, thirdly, the Party, as the best school for training leaders of the working class, is, by reason of its experience and prestige, the only organisation capable of centralising the leadership of the struggle of the proletariat, thus transforming each and every non-Party organisation of the working class into an auxiliary body and transmission belt linking the Party with the class.

The Party is the highest form of class organisation of the proletariat.

This does not mean, of course, that non-Party organisations, trade unions, co-operatives, etc., should be officially subordinated to the Party leadership. It only means that the members of the Party who belong to these organisations and are doubtlessly influential in them should do all they can to persuade these non-Party organisations to draw nearer to the Party of the proletariat in their work and voluntarily accept its political leadership.

That is why Lenin says that the Party is "the *highest* form of proletarian class association," whose political leadership must extend to every other form of organization of the proletariat (see Vol. XXV, p. 194).[*]

That is why the opportunist theory of the "independence" and "neutrality" of the non-Party organisations, which breeds *independent* members of parliament and journalists *isolated* from the Party, *narrow-minded* trade union leaders and *philistine* co-operative officials, is wholly incompatible with the theory and practice of Leninism.

4) *The Party as an instrument of the dictatorship of the proletariat.* The Party is the highest form of organisation of the proletariat. The Party is the principle guiding force within the class of the proletarians and among the organisations of that class. But it does not by any means follow from this that the Party can be regarded as an end in itself, as a self-sufficient force. The Party is not only the highest form of class association of the proletarians; it is at the same time an *instrument* in the hands of the proletariat *for* achieving the dictatorship, when that has not yet been achieved and *for* consolidating and expanding the dictatorship when it has already been achieved. The Party could not have risen so high in importance and could not have exerted its influence over all other forms of organisations of the proletariat, if the latter had not been confronted with the question of power, if the conditions of imperialism, the inevitability of wars, and the existence of a crisis had not yet de-

---

[*] " 'Left-Wing' Communism, an Infantile Disorder."

103

manded the concentration of all the forces of the proletariat at one point, the gathering of all the threads of the revolutionary movement in one spot in order to overthrow the bourgeoisie and to achieve the dictatorship of the proletariat. The proletariat needs the Party first of all as its General Staff, which it must have for the successful seizure of power. It scarcely needs proof that without a party capable of rallying around itself the mass organisations of the proletariat, and of centralising the leadership of the entire movement during the progress of the struggle, the proletariat in Russia could not have established its revolutionary dictatorship.

But the proletariat needs the Party not only to achieve the dictatorship; it needs it still more to maintain the dictatorship, to consolidate and expand it in order to achieve the complete victory of socialism.

"Certainly, almost everyone now realises," says Lenin, "that the Bolsheviks could not have maintained themselves in power for two-and-a-half months, let alone two-and-a-half years, without the strictest, truly iron discipline in our Party, and without the fullest and unreserved support of the latter by the whole mass of the working class, that is, by all its thinking, honest, self-sacrificing and influential elements, capable of leading or of carrying with them the backwards strata" (see Vol. XXV, p. 173).[*]

Now, what does to "maintain" and "expand" the dictatorship mean? It means imbuing the millions of proletarians with the spirit of discipline and organisation; it means creating among the proletarian masses a cementing force and a bulwark against the corrosive influence of the petty-bourgeois elemental forces and petty-bourgeois habits; it means enhancing the organising work of the proletarians in re-educating and remoulding the petty-bourgeois strata; it means helping the masses of the proletarians to educate themselves as a force capable of

---

[*] Ibid.

abolishing classes and of preparing the conditions for the organisation of socialist production. But it is impossible to accomplish all this without a party which is strong by reason of its solidarity and discipline.

"The dictatorship of the proletariat," says Lenin, "is a stubborn struggle – bloody and bloodless, violent and peaceful, military and economic, educational and administrative – against the forces and traditions of the old society. The force of habit of millions and tens of millions is a most terrible force. Without an iron party tempered in the struggle, without a party enjoying the confidence of all that is honest in the given class, without a party capable of watching and influencing the mood of the masses, it is impossible to conduct such a strategy successfully" (see Vol. XXV, p. 190).[*]

The proletariat needs the Party *for* the purpose of achieving and maintaining the dictatorship. The Party is an instrument of the dictatorship of the proletariat.

But from this it follows that when classes disappear and the dictatorship of the proletariat withers away, the Party also will wither away.

5) *The Party as the embodiment of unity of will, unity incompatible with the existence of factions.* The achievement and maintenance of the dictatorship of the proletariat is impossible without a party which is strong by reason of its solidarity and iron discipline. But iron discipline in the Party is inconceivable without unity of will, without complete and absolute unity of action on the part of all members of the Party. This does not mean, of course, that the possibility of conflicts of opinion within the Party is thereby precluded. On the contrary, iron discipline does not preclude but presupposes criticism and conflict of opinion within the Party. Least of all does it mean that discipline must be "blind." On the contrary, iron discipline does not preclude but presupposes conscious and voluntary submission,

---

[*] Ibid.

for only conscious discipline can be truly iron discipline. But after a conflict of opinion has been closed, after criticism has been exhausted and a decision has been arrived at, unity of will and unity of action of all Party members are the necessary conditions without which neither Party unity nor iron discipline in the Party is conceivable.

"In the present epoch of acute civil war," says Lenin, "the Communist Party will be able to perform its duty only if it is organised in the most centralised manner, if iron discipline bordering on military discipline prevails in it, and if its Party centre is a powerful and authoritative organ, wielding wide powers and enjoying the universal confidence of the members of the Party" (see Vol. XXV, pp. 282-83).[*]

This is the position in regard to discipline in the Party in the period of struggle preceding the achievement of the dictatorship.

The same, but to an even greater degree, must be said about discipline in the Party after the dictatorship has been achieved.

"Whoever," says Lenin, "weakens in the least the iron discipline of the Party of the proletariat (especially during the time of its dictatorship), actually aids the bourgeoisie against the proletariat" (see Vol. XXV, p. 190).[†]

But from this it follows that the existence of factions is compatible neither with the Party's unity nor with its iron discipline. It scarcely needs proof that the existence of factions leads to the existence of a number of centres, and the existence of a number of centres means the absence of one common centre in the Party, the breaking up of unity of will, the weakening and disintegration of discipline, the weakening and disintegration of the dictatorship. Of course, the parties of the Second International, which are fighting against the dictatorship of the prole-

---

[*] "The Terms of Admission into the Communist International," July 1920.
[†] " 'Left-Wing' Communism, an Infantile Disorder."

tariat and have no desire to lead the proletarians to power, can afford such liberalism as freedom of factions, for they have no need at all for iron discipline. But the parties of the Communist International, whose activities are conditioned by the task of achieving and consolidating the dictatorship of the proletariat, cannot afford to be "liberal" or to permit freedom of factions.

The Party represents unity of will, which precludes all factionalism and division of authority in the Party.

Hence Lenin's warning about the "danger of factionalism from the point of view of Party unity and of effecting the unity of will of the vanguard of the proletariat as the fundamental condition for the success of the dictatorship of the proletariat," which is embodied in the special resolution of the Tenth Congress of our Party "On Party Unity."[22]

Hence Lenin's demand for the "complete elimination of all factionalism" and the "immediate dissolution of all groups, without exemption, that have been formed on the basis of various platforms," on pain of "unconditional and immediate expulsion from the Party" (see the resolution "On Party Unity").

6) *The Party becomes strong by purging itself of opportunist elements.* The source of factionalism in the Party is its opportunist elements. The proletariat is not an isolated class. It is consistently replenished by the influx of peasants, petty bourgeois and intellectuals proletarianised by the development of capitalism. At the same time the upper stratum of the proletariat, principally trade union leaders and members of parliament who are fed by the bourgeoisie out of the super-profits extracted from the colonies, is undergoing a process of decay. "This stratum of bourgeoisified workers, or the 'labour aristocracy'," says Lenin, "who are quite philistine in their mode of life, in the size of their earnings and in their entire outlook, is the principal prop of the Second International, and, in our days, the principal *social* (not military) *prop of the bourgeoisie.* For they are real *agents of the bourgeoisie in the working-class* movement, the

labour lieutenants of the capitalist class, real channels of reformism and chauvinism" (see Vol. XIX, p. 77).[*]

In one way or another, all these petty-bourgeois groups penetrate into the Party and introduce into it the spirit of hesitancy and opportunism, the spirit of demoralization and uncertainty. It is they, principally, that constitute the source of factionalism and disintegration, the source of disorganisation and disruption of the Party from within. To fight imperialism with such "allies" in one's rear means to put oneself in the position of being caught between two fires, from the front and from the rear. Therefore, ruthless struggle against such elements, their expulsion from the Party, is a pre-requisite for the successful struggle against imperialism.

The theory of "defeating" opportunist elements by the ideological struggle within the Party, the theory of "overcoming" these elements within the confines of a single party, is a rotten and dangerous theory, which threatens to condemn the Party to paralysis and chronic infirmity, threatens to leave the Party a prey to opportunism, threatens to leave the proletariat without a revolutionary party, threatens to deprive the proletariat of its main weapon in the fight against imperialism. Our Party could not have emerged on to the broad highway, it could not have seized power and organised the dictatorship of the proletariat, it could not have emerged victorious from the civil war, if it had had within its ranks people like Martov and Dan, Potresov and Axelrod. Our Party succeeded in achieving internal unity and unexampled cohesion of its ranks primarily because it was able in good time to purge itself of the opportunist pollution, because it was able to rid its ranks of the Liquidators and Mensheviks. Proletarian parties develop and become strong by purging themselves of opportunists and reformists, social-

---

[*] "Preface to the French and German Editions of *Imperialism, the Highest Stage of Capitalism*," July 1920.

imperialists and social-chauvinists, social-patriots and social-pacifists.

The Party becomes strong by purging itself of opportunist elements.

"With reformists, Mensheviks, in our ranks," says Lenin, "it is *impossible* to be victorious in the proletarian revolution, it is *impossible* to defend it. That is obvious in principle, and it has been strikingly confirmed by the experience of both Russia and Hungary.... In Russia, difficult situations have arisen *many times*, when the Soviet regime would *most certainly* have been overthrown had Mensheviks, reformists and petty-bourgeois democrats remained in our Party... In Italy, where, as is generally admitted, decisive battles between the proletariat and the bourgeoisie for the possession of state power are imminent. At such a moment it is not only absolutely necessary to remove the Mensheviks, reformists, Turatists from the Party, but it may even be useful to remove excellent Communists who are liable to waver, and who reveal a tendency to waver towards 'unity' with the reformists, to remove them from all responsible posts.... On the eve of a revolution, and at a moment when a most fierce struggle is being waged for its victory, the slightest wavering in the ranks of the Party may *wreck everything*, frustrate the revolution, wrest the power from the hands of the proletariat; for this power is not yet consolidated, the attack upon it is still very strong. The desertion of wavering leaders at such a time does not weaken but strengthens the Party, the working-class movement and the revolution" (see Vol. XXV, pp. 462, 463, 464).[*]

---

[*] "On the Struggle Within the Italian Socialist Party," November 1920.

IX

STYLE IN WORK

I am not referring to literary style. What I have in mind is style in work, that specific and peculiar feature in the practice of Leninism which creates the special type of Leninist worker. Leninism is a school of theory and practice which trains a special type of Party and state worker, creates a special Leninist style in work.

What are the characteristic features of this style? What are its peculiarities?

It has two specific features:

a) Russian revolutionary sweep and

b) American efficiency.

The style of Leninism consists in combining these two specific features in Party and state work.

Russian revolutionary sweep is an antidote to inertia, routine, conservationism, mental stagnation and slavish submission to ancient traditions. Russian revolutionary sweep is the life-giving force which stimulates thought, impels things forward, breaks the past and opens up perspectives. Without it no progress is possible.

But Russian revolutionary sweep has every chance of degenerating in practice into empty "revolutionary" Manilovism if it is not combined with American efficiency in work. Examples of this degeneration are only too numerous. Who does not know the disease of "revolutionary" scheme concocting and "revolutionary" plan drafting, which springs from the belief in the power of decrees to arrange everything and re-make everything? A Russian writer, I. Ehrenburg, in his story *The Percommon* (*The Perfect Communist Man*), has portrayed the type of a "Bolshevik" afflicted with this disease, who set himself the task of finding a formula for the ideally perfect man and... became "submerged" in this "work." The story contains a great exaggeration, but it certainly gives a correct likeness of the disease. But no one, I think, has so ruthlessly and bitterly ridiculed those afflicted with this disease as Lenin. Lenin stigmatised this morbid belief in concocting schemes and in turning out decrees as "communist vainglory."

"Communist vainglory," says Lenin, "means that a man, who is a member of the Communist Party, and has not yet been purged from it, imagines that he can solve all his problems by issuing communist decrees" (see Vol. XXVII, pp. 50-51).[*]

Lenin usually contrasted hollow "revolutionary" phrasemongering with plain everyday work, thus emphasising that "revolutionary" scheme concocting is repugnant to the spirit and the letter of true Leninism.

"Fewer pompous phrases, more plain, *everyday* work...," says Lenin.
"Less political fireworks and more attention to the simplest but vital... facts of communist construction..." (see Vol. XXIV, pp. 343 and 335).[†]

American efficiency, on the other hand, is an antidote to "revolutionary" Manilovism and fantastic scheme concocting. American efficiency is that indomitable force which neither knows nor recognises obstacles; which with its business-like perseverance brushes aside all obstacles; which continues at a task once started until it is finished, even if it is a minor task; and without which serious constructive work is inconceivable.

---

[*] "The New Economic Policy and the Tasks of the Political Education Departments," October 1921.
[†] "A Great Beginning," June 1919.

But American efficiency has every chance of degenerating into narrow and unprincipled practicalism if it is not combined with Russian revolutionary sweep. Who has not heard of that disease of narrow empiricism and unprincipled practicalism which has not infrequently caused certain "Bolsheviks" to degenerate and to abandon the cause of the revolution? We find a reflection of this peculiar disease in a story by B. Pilnyak, entitled *The Barren Year*, which depicts types of Russian "Bolsheviks" of strong will and practical determination who "function" very "energetically," but without vision, without knowing "what it is all about," and who, therefore, stray from the path of revolutionary work. No one has ridiculed this disease of practicalism so incisively as Lenin. He branded it as "narrow-minded empiricism" and "brainless practicalism." He usually contrasted it with vital revolutionary work and the necessity of having a revolutionary perspective in all our daily activities, thus emphasising that this unprincipled practicalism is as repugnant to true Leninism as "revolutionary" scheme concocting.

The combination of Russian revolutionary sweep with American efficiency is the essence of Leninism in Party and state work.

This combination alone produces the finished type of Leninist worker, the style of Leninism in work.

Pravda, Nos. 96, 97, 103, 105, 107, 108, 111;
April 26 and 30,
May 9, 11, 14, 15 and 18, 1924

NOTES

[1] J. V. Stalin's lectures, "The Foundations of Leninism," were published in *Pravda* in April and May 1924. In May 1924, Stalin's pamphlet *On Lenin and Leninism* appeared, containing his reminiscences of Lenin and the lectures "The Foundations of Leninism." These lectures are included in all the editions of his book *Problems of Leninism.*

[2] Marx and Engels, *Manifesto of the Communist Party*, Foreign Languages Press, Peking, 1973, p. 76.   p. 9

[3] This refers to the statement by Marx in his letter to Engels of April 16, 1856. (See Marx and Engels, *Selected Works*, Foreign Languages Publishing House, Moscow, 1951, Vol. II, p. 412.)   p. 14

[4] This refers to Engels' article "The Bakuninists at Work." (See Marx and Engels, *Collected Works*, Ger. ed., Dietz Verlag, Berlin, 1962, Vol. 18, pp. 476-93.)   p. 15

[5] Lenin, *"Left-Wing" Communism, an Infantile Disorder*, FLP, Peking, 1970, p. 7.   p. 16

[6] See Lenin, *What the "Friends of the People" Are and How They Fight the Social-Democrats*, FLPH, Moscow, 1950, pp. 251-52.   p. 16

[7] *The Basle Congress of the Second International* was held November 24-25, 1912. It was convened in connection with the Balkan War and the impending threat of a world war. Only one question was discussed: the international situation and joint action against war. The congress adopted a manifesto calling upon the workers to utilize the organization and might of the proletariat to wage a revolutionary struggle against the danger of war, to declare "war against war."   p. 16

[8] See Marx, "Afterword to the Second German Edition," *Capital*, FLPH, Moscow, 1954, Vol. I, p. 20.   p. 18

[9] Engels, "Ludwig Feuerbach and the End of Classical German Philosophy." (Marx and Engels, *Selected Works*, FLPH, Moscow, 1951, Vol. II, p. 338.)   p. 20

[10] See Marx, "Theses on Feuerbach." (Marx and Engels, *Selected Works*, FLPH. Moscow, 1951, Vol. II, p. 367.)   p. 22

[11] See Lenin, *Imperialism, the Highest Stage of Capitalism*, FLP. Peking, 1973.   p. 23

[12] Stalin refers to the writings by Lenin in 1905, namely, "Social-Democracy and the Provisional Revolutionary Government," from which he cites a passage; "The Revolutionary Democratic-Dictatorship of the Proletariat and the Peasantry"; and "On the Provisional Revolutionary Government." (See Lenin, *Works*, 4th Russ. ed., Vol. 8, pp. 247-63, 264-74 and 427-47.)   p. 30

[13] Marx and Engels, "Address of the Central Committee to the Communist League," *Selected Works*, FLPH, Moscow, 1951, Vol. I, p. 102.   p. 33

[14] A Russian saying carried over from the Russo-Turkish War of 1877-78. There was heavy fighting at the Shipka Pass, but the tsarist headquarters in their communiqués reported: "All quiet at the Shipka Pass."   p. 42

[15] Marx and Engels, "Preface to the German Edition of 1872," *Manifesto of the Communist Party*, FLP, Peking, 1973, p. 2; *Selected Works*, FLPH, Moscow, 1951, Vol. II, p. 420.   p. 44

[16] See Engels, "The Peasant Question in France and Germany." (Marx and Engels, *Selected Works*, FLPH, Moscow, 1951, Vol. II, p. 382.)   p. 61

[17] *Ibid.*, pp. 394-95.   p. 61

[18] *Selskosoyuz* – the All-Russian Union of Rural Co-operatives – existed from August 1921 to June 1929.   p. 63

[19] Wolfgang Kapp (1868-1922) was the ringleader of the counter-revolutionary coup d'état of 1920 in Germany, which was known as the "Kapp putsch." He became the head of a new short-lived government which was overthrown by the general strike of the German workers.   p. 88

[20] See Lenin, "The Importance of Gold Now and After the Complete Victory of Socialism," *Selected Works*, FLPH, Moscow, 1952, Vol. II, Part 2, pp. 603-11.   p. 92

[21] *Manilovism* – smug complacency, futile daydreaming; from the landowner Manilov, a character in Gogol's *Dead Souls*.   p. 98

[22] The resolution "On Party Unity" was written by Lenin and adopted by the Tenth Congress of the R.C.P.(B.), held March 8-16, 1921. (See Lenin, *Selected Works*, FLPH, Moscow, 1952, Vol. II, Part 2, pp. 497-501, and also *Resolutions and Decisions of C.P.S.U. (B.) Congresses, Conferences and Central Committee Plenums*, in Russian, 1941, Part I, pp. 364-66.)   p. 107

Made in the USA
Las Vegas, NV
06 December 2022

61009057R00075